ANXI

ATTACHMENT

RECOVERY

A Personal Growth and Development Guide to Building Secure Attachment, Trust, Emotional Intelligence, Communication, and Boundaries in Relationships

RICHARD BANKS

Why You Should Read This Book

Are you tired of feeling like you're walking on eggshells in your relationships? Do you find yourself overanalyzing every text, every interaction, every slight change in your partner's tone? Does the fear of rejection or abandonment keep you from fully opening your heart?

If this resonates with you, you're not alone. Anxious attachment is a common struggle, but it doesn't have to define your love life. **"Anxious Attachment Recovery"** is your guide to breaking free from the emotional cycle of insecurity and building the secure, loving relationships you deserve.

Whether you're single, dating, or in a long-term relationship, this book is designed to meet you where you are and guide you toward greater emotional security.

- **If you're single,** learn how to cultivate the self-love and emotional resilience needed to attract healthy relationships, breaking free from old patterns of anxious attachment.
- **If you're dating,** discover how to navigate new relationships with confidence by setting healthy boundaries and

communicating your needs effectively—without fear of conflict.

- **If you're in a committed relationship,** find strategies to strengthen your connection, overcome challenges, and build a partnership founded on trust, mutual respect, and emotional intimacy.

Here's a glimpse of what you'll discover within these pages:

- Unraveling the Past: We'll delve into your childhood experiences, exploring how early relationships with caregivers can shape your attachment style and influence your present-day connections. You'll gain profound insights into why you react the way you do, freeing you from self-blame and empowering you to move forward.
- Taming the Inner Critic: That voice inside your head that whispers doubts and fears? We'll help you quiet it down. You'll learn to challenge negative thoughts, replace self-criticism with self-compassion, and cultivate a more positive and empowering inner dialogue.
- Mastering Your Emotions: Feelings of anxiety, jealousy, and insecurity can feel overwhelming. This book will equip you with practical techniques to regulate your emotions, find inner calm, and respond to challenges with grace and resilience.

Imagine feeling centered and grounded, even in the face of relationship stressors.

- Finding Your Voice: Learn to communicate your needs and boundaries with clarity and confidence. We'll explore assertive communication strategies, helping you express yourself authentically without fear of conflict or rejection. You'll discover the power of open, honest dialogue to build deeper connections.
- Building Trust and Security: Trust is the foundation of any healthy relationship. We'll guide you on a journey to rebuild trust, both in yourself and in others. You'll learn to recognize red flags, set healthy boundaries, and cultivate relationships that foster safety and security.
- Embracing Self-Love: True healing begins with self-acceptance. This book will empower you to reclaim your self-worth, embrace your strengths, and cultivate a deep sense of love and compassion for yourself. You'll discover that the most important relationship you'll ever have is the one with yourself.

Above all, **"Anxious Attachment Recovery"** empowers you to reclaim your self-worth. It teaches you to embrace your strengths, foster self-love, and discover that the most important relationship you'll ever have is with yourself.

You deserve to experience love that nourishes your soul, not drains your energy. You deserve to feel safe, secure, and cherished. This book is your invitation to step into that reality.

Your journey to lasting love and emotional freedom begins today. Take the first step, buy the book, and start transforming your relationships.

Thank You!

Thank you for your purchase.

I am dedicated to making the most enriching and informational content. I hope it meets your expectations and you gain a lot from it.

Your comments and feedback are important to me because they help me to provide the best material possible. So, if you have any questions or concerns, please email me at richard@richardbanks.cc

Again, thank you for your purchase.

.

INTRODUCTION: BREAKING FREE FROM ANXIOUS ATTACHMENT

Do you lie awake at night, your mind filled with worries about your relationships? Does your heart race with anxiety at the slightest hint of distance or disapproval from your loved ones? Do you constantly seek reassurance, only to be troubled by a lingering sense of insecurity? If this sounds familiar, you're not alone.

Millions of people struggle with anxious attachment, leaving them to feel trapped in a recurring cycle of fear, insecurity, and emotional turmoil. This attachment style can affect every aspect of your life, from your romantic relationships to your friendships, family dynamics, and even professional interactions. It can rob you of joy, peace, and the confidence to pursue your dreams.

But here's the empowering truth: *you don't have to live this way.* Healing is possible. You can break free from the grip of anxious attachment and create a life filled with secure love, lasting confidence, and deep, fulfilling connections.

I understand the pain of anxious attachment firsthand. For years, I was held captive by the fear of abandonment and rejection. My happiness hinged on the approval of others, and I would go to great lengths to avoid any hint of disapproval. It was an exhausting and isolating way to live.

But I soon discovered a path to freedom. Through therapy, self-reflection, and the unwavering support of loved ones, I embarked on a journey of transformation. I learned to rewire my thinking, manage my emotions, and cultivate healthy relationship patterns. It wasn't easy, but it was the most rewarding experience of my life.

Today, I stand before you as living proof that recovery from anxious attachment is possible. Fear or insecurity no longer control me. I've built strong, secure relationships based on trust and mutual respect. And most importantly, I've reclaimed my sense of self-worth and discovered the joy of emotional freedom.

This practical, actionable guide is your roadmap to that same freedom. It will help you to:

- Understand the Roots of Your Anxiety: We'll explore how early childhood experiences can shape your attachment style and contribute to your current struggles. Understanding where your anxiety comes from is the first step toward healing it.
- Identify Your Triggers: You'll learn to recognize the specific situations, behaviors, and thoughts that trigger your anxious feelings. This self-awareness is crucial for breaking free from reactive patterns.
- Challenge Negative Beliefs: We'll work on replacing self-doubting thoughts with more positive and empowering affirmations. You'll

learn to cultivate a mindset of self-compassion and resilience.

- Develop Emotional Regulation Skills: You'll discover powerful techniques to manage your emotions effectively, reducing your reliance on external validation and building inner strength.
- Communicate with Confidence and Clarity: You'll learn to express your needs and boundaries clearly and assertively, fostering healthier and more balanced relationships.
- Build Healthy Relationships: We'll identify strategies for nurturing strong, secure connections with loved ones based on trust, mutual respect, and emotional intimacy.

Healing from anxious attachment goes beyond managing anxiety. It allows you to create a life full of joy, peace, and contentment. Imagine:

- Waking up each morning with a sense of calm and confidence, free from the weight of worry and insecurity.

- Experiencing deep, fulfilling relationships where you feel safe, loved, and valued for who you are.
- Embracing emotional independence and the freedom to pursue your dreams without fear of rejection or abandonment.
- Living a purposeful, passionate, and a peacefully profound life.

This is the life that awaits you on the other side of anxious attachment. A life where you're no longer defined by your fears but by your strengths, resilience, and capacity for love and connection.

Understanding Anxious Attachment

Before we begin this transformative journey, let's take a closer look at what anxious attachment looks like and how it impacts your life.

Anxious attachment is characterized by an overwhelming fear of being abandoned or rejected. This fear can lead to behaviors that seek constant reassurance from loved ones. You may find yourself:

- Questioning the strength of your relationships
- Seeking validation through frequent communication
- Feeling anxious when your partner or loved one is unavailable

While these behaviors are attempts to feel secure, they often lead to feelings of insecurity, emotional highs and lows, and even conflict within your relationships. This attachment style typically stems from early childhood experiences, often due to inconsistent caregiving. These past experiences create a blueprint for how you approach relationships in adulthood. If you've been following this blueprint, you likely feel the need to keep relationships "safe" by being hypervigilant and constantly seeking reassurance that you are loved, valued, and important to those around you.

In my previous book, *"Anxious Attachment and Avoidant Detachment",* we examined the concepts of anxious and avoidant attachment, exploring how these patterns form, how they affect our relationships, and why they lead to emotional turmoil.

This book picks up where we left off, but instead of just understanding anxious attachment, we'll focus on how to move beyond it. This is your guide to recovery—a practical, actionable path that helps you transition from anxious attachment to emotional security.

Why Recovery Is Possible

If you've lived with anxious attachment for most of your life, you might feel like it's an ingrained part of your personality. But the truth is, your brain is incredibly adaptable. Through neuroplasticity—the brain's ability to reorganize itself by forming new neural connections—you can create new patterns of thinking and behaving that support secure attachment.

This book is a valuable resource for rewiring your brain and transforming your relationships. It's packed with practical exercises, insightful reflections, and proven strategies to help you shift your mindset, challenge your limiting beliefs, and step into a more confident, secure version of yourself. By harnessing the power of neuroplasticity, these tools will empower you to create new, secure patterns of relating and break free from the grip of anxious attachment.

The chapters ahead will offer practical strategies to help you recognize your emotional triggers, reframe your internal dialogue, and build healthier relationship habits. You'll learn how to rewrite the anxious narratives that run through your mind, manage your need for reassurance, and overcome the fear of abandonment that fuels so much of your anxiety.

This book will guide you step-by-step through the process of understanding and transforming your attachment patterns.

We will:

- Delve into the roots of your anxiety, uncovering how early experiences shaped your attachment style
- Identify the specific triggers that cause your anxious behaviors in relationships
- Explore strategies for shifting your mindset from anxious to secure

- Learn emotional self-regulation techniques to manage intense emotions and reduce reliance on external reassurance
- Develop assertive communication skills to express your needs and boundaries confidently
- Learn how to build secure relationships, whether you're single, dating, or in a committed partnership

This Book Is for You, No Matter Where You Are on Your Journey

Whether you're single, dating, or in a long-term relationship, this book is designed to meet you where you are and guide you toward greater emotional security.

- If you're single, learn how to develop self-love and emotional resilience needed to attract healthy relationships and avoid repeating patterns of anxious attachment.
- If you're dating, discover how to navigate new relationships with confidence by setting healthy boundaries, and communicating your needs effectively.

- If you're in a committed relationship, find strategies to strengthen your connection, overcome challenges, and create a partnership built on trust, mutual respect, and emotional intimacy.

Please take a moment to acknowledge the incredible strength and courage it takes to confront your attachment patterns and commit to change. I believe everyone deserves to live a life free from anxiety and insecurity. This is your moment to break free from the grip of anxiety and step into a life of greater love, confidence, and connection.

You're not alone. You're capable of healing. And this book is here to guide you every step of the way.

Let's begin.

CHAPTER 1: UNDERSTANDING THE ROOTS OF YOUR ANXIETY

Anxious attachment doesn't develop overnight. It's the culmination of years of learned behavior, experiences, and emotional responses deeply rooted in your earliest relationships. If you struggle with anxious attachment, you may constantly question whether you're loved or valued, and that uncertainty can manifest in intense emotional reactions. This attachment style is a deeply ingrained pattern that can affect all your relationships, from family and friends to coworkers, not just romantic partners.

In this chapter, we'll discuss the development of anxious attachment, the impact of early life experiences on current relational patterns, and how understanding your personal attachment history can be the first step toward healing. Recognizing these emotional patterns can empower you to take control of your reactions, identify the root causes of your anxiety, and set the stage for your recovery.

WHY ANXIOUS ATTACHMENT DEVELOPS

Anxious attachment often begins in early childhood. The way your caregivers interacted with you—whether they were nurturing and consistent or distant and unpredictable—profoundly impacts your self-perception and relationships with others.

Children need a reliable source of love, security, and support to feel safe in their environment. When these needs are met inconsistently, the child learns that love and security are not guaranteed, creating a foundation for anxious attachment.

28

If your caregivers were sometimes emotionally available but other times neglectful or preoccupied, it created a sense of unpredictability in your young mind. One day, your parents may have been affectionate and attentive, but the next, they may have been distant or emotionally unavailable. This inconsistency teaches children that love and validation must be sought after and that emotional connection can be easily lost.

You may have learned to be hypervigilant—constantly on the lookout for signs that love or care was being withdrawn. This hypervigilance becomes internalized, and as you grow older, you carry this pattern into adult relationships. The need for constant validation, fear of abandonment, and anxiety around emotional distance are all reflections of that early uncertainty.

THE ROLE OF CAREGIVERS AND ENVIRONMENT

Anxious attachment is also shaped by the environment in which you grew up. For example, if your parents or caregivers were dealing with their own stress—perhaps financial struggles, personal issues, or emotional unavailability—they may have been less able to provide the consistent love and care you needed.

29

In some cases, anxious attachment develops in households where caregivers are loving but overprotective, causing a child to grow up feeling emotionally dependent on external validation. It's also worth noting that cultural and societal factors play a role. In some cultures, emotional expression is discouraged, and children are taught to suppress their feelings. This lack of emotional support can foster a sense of emotional insecurity, contributing to anxious attachment in adulthood.

As an adult, these early experiences may lead you to question your worth and whether you deserve love. You might constantly seek validation from your partner, fearing that their affection could disappear at any moment. Your fears are a result of your early experiences, not simply irrational thoughts.

THE NEUROBIOLOGY OF ANXIOUS ATTACHMENT: UNDERSTANDING THE BRAIN'S RESPONSE

While anxious attachment is rooted in early experiences, it also affects how your brain responds to emotional stimuli in relationships. When you feel anxious or uncertain about your partner's feelings, your brain is triggered into a heightened state of alertness—commonly referred to as the "fight or flight" response.

Imagine this: You send your partner a message, and hours go by without a response. As time passes, your anxiety builds. Your heart races, your stomach tightens, and a flood of thoughts takes over: What if they're upset with me? What if they've lost interest?

What's happening here is that your brain is interpreting the lack of communication as a threat to your emotional security. This triggers the amygdala, which is part of the brain responsible for processing fear and anxiety, to sound the alarm. The amygdala then signals the hypothalamus to release stress hormones like cortisol and adrenaline, preparing your body for the fight-or-flight response.

In relationships, this "threat" isn't physical but emotional. Your brain treats your partner's delayed response the same way it would treat a potential danger in your environment. The anxiety you feel is your brain's way of protecting you from what it perceives as a potential loss of connection.

At this moment, the prefrontal cortex—the rational part of your brain responsible for logical thinking—is struggling to keep up. Its role is to moderate the amygdala's response, reminding you that your partner could simply be busy and not deliberately ignoring you. However, in moments of intense anxiety, the emotional brain overpowers the rational brain. This is why, even though a part of you might know nothing is wrong, you might still feel overwhelmed and resort to compulsively checking your phone or sending another message for reassurance.

This pattern is a direct reflection of your early attachment experiences. Your brain is wired to expect inconsistency, so it reacts strongly to any perceived signs of emotional distance. The key here is that this neurobiological response, while powerful, is not set in stone.

REWIRING YOUR BRAIN'S RESPONSE

The good news is that your brain has the ability to change. Through neuroplasticity, the brain can form new pathways that support healthier, more secure responses to emotional uncertainty. This means that, over time, you can train your brain to react differently when faced with situations that trigger your anxiety.

For example, when you notice the familiar surge of panic after a delayed text response, take a moment to pause and breathe deeply. This gives your prefrontal cortex the opportunity to catch up with your emotional response, allowing you to think more clearly. Instead of immediately assuming the worst, you can remind yourself: "My partner is likely just busy right now; this doesn't mean anything about their feelings for me."

By consistently practicing this kind of self-regulation, you can begin to change the way your brain processes

33

these moments. Eventually, you'll find that your anxiety diminishes, and you can approach relationships from a place of trust rather than fear. This rewiring process is a powerful tool in overcoming anxious attachment and developing a more secure sense of self in relationships.

Now that we understand the brain's role in anxious attachment, let's explore how your personal history has shaped your unique patterns and beliefs.

EXPLORING YOUR PERSONAL ATTACHMENT HISTORY

Reflection is an essential part in the process of healing from anxious attachment. By taking time to look back on your early attachment experiences, you gain a better understanding of how those formative years have shaped your current relationship dynamics. The way our caregivers—whether parents, guardians, or other influential adults—responded to our emotional needs can affect how we relate to others as adults.

34

Anxious attachment is often rooted in inconsistent or unpredictable caregiving, leading to a deep-seated fear of abandonment and a craving for validation and security.

Going through this reflective process can be both enlightening and emotionally challenging. As you begin to uncover the roots of your anxious attachment, it's important to approach yourself with compassion and understanding. Keep in mind that your attachment style is not a flaw or a failure. Instead, it's a learned response, shaped by your early experiences. By reflecting on those experiences, you're taking the first crucial step in changing the patterns that no longer benefit you.

EXERCISE: REFLECTING ON YOUR EARLY ATTACHMENT EXPERIENCES

1. **How did your caregivers respond to your emotional needs?**

This question asks you to revisit your earliest

relationships. Reflect on how your caregivers— whether they were your parents, grandparents, or other close figures—handled your emotional needs. Were they consistently available and nurturing, or were there moments when they seemed distant, distracted, or emotionally unavailable? Try to recall moments when you needed comfort or validation as a child. Did they hold you and provide soothing words, or did they dismiss your feelings, leaving you feeling emotionally neglected?

As we've mentioned earlier, inconsistent caregiving often plays a major role in the development of anxious attachment. If your caregivers were sometimes available but other times distant, you may have learned to become hypervigilant, always seeking security and fearing that you would be left alone. This inconsistency teaches children that love and attention are unpredictable, leading to a sense of insecurity that follows them into adulthood.

2. Did you feel secure in your relationships with your caregivers, or were there moments of doubt?

Think back to your childhood. Did you feel safe, secure, and confident in your relationships with your caregivers, or were there moments of doubt and uncertainty? If you've ever experienced moments of doubt, you might have questioned if you were loved, if you could rely on your caregivers, or if you had to earn their attention by behaving in certain ways. Insecure relationships during childhood can lead to anxious behaviors in adulthood, where you constantly seek validation and reassurance, fearing that love might be withdrawn at any moment.

Children who experience doubt in their relationships often develop anxious tendencies—worrying about whether they are good enough and lovable, and if they will be abandoned for not meeting certain expectations. Understanding these early doubts can help you identify why you

37

may seek constant validation in your current relationships.

3. How did you react when you felt neglected or ignored as a child?

When you felt emotionally neglected or ignored, how did you respond? Did you try to gain attention through specific behaviors, such as acting out, withdrawing, or becoming overly compliant? Did you feel a deep sense of anxiety or worry when your caregivers weren't responsive to your emotional needs?

Children who feel neglected often develop coping mechanisms to get the attention they crave. While helpful in childhood, these coping mechanisms can become maladaptive in adulthood. For example, you may have learned to become overly accommodating or compliant to gain approval, or you may have developed anxious behaviors such as excessive people-pleasing, overthinking, or becoming emotionally clingy in relationships.

Recognizing these patterns allows you to understand how they continue to influence your adult relationships.

4. How do these early experiences show up in your current relationships?

Now that you've reflected on your childhood experiences, it's time to connect the dots to your adult relationships. Do you see patterns of seeking validation, fear of abandonment, or overthinking in your romantic or platonic relationships? Are there times when you feel anxious or worried that your partner or friend will leave you, even when there is no immediate reason to think so? Do you find yourself overanalyzing their actions or words, searching for signs of rejection or abandonment?

By identifying these patterns, you can begin to see your anxious attachment tendencies not as personal flaws but as **learned responses** from your past. These behaviors were your way of navigating inconsistent caregiving, but they may

39

no longer serve you in healthy relationships. Recognizing the connections between your past and present is the first step toward breaking free from anxious attachment.

UNDERSTANDING THE LINK BETWEEN PAST AND PRESENT

It's crucial to remember that anxious attachment patterns were not created overnight, nor will they disappear overnight. These patterns were shaped by years of early experiences that have left a lasting imprint on your emotional responses. By reflecting on your personal attachment history, you now have the power to rewrite your narrative. You can see the origin of these behaviors, and with that awareness comes the ability to change them.

Reflection is a tool that will guide you throughout your journey to emotional freedom. As you move forward in this book and explore strategies for healing and building more secure attachments, continue to revisit your reflections. The more you

you do, you feel that it's never enough to maintain a secure connection with your partner. You might feel like you have to be "more"—more attractive, more attentive, more everything—just to hold on to love.

- **""I have to work hard to be loved."**

Those with anxious attachment often internalize the idea that love must be earned, leading them to overcompensate in relationships. You might go out of your way to please your partner, even at the expense of your own needs and boundaries, hoping this will secure their love and commitment.

- **"If I don't constantly prove my worth, my partner will leave me."**

This belief fosters a fear-based approach to relationships. You may feel that unless you constantly show your partner how valuable you are—by doing things for them, giving them attention, or accommodating their needs—they will eventually lose interest and abandon you.

- **"I am not worthy of lasting love."**

  At its core, anxious attachment can make you feel unlovable or undeserving of lasting, secure affection. This belief can make it difficult to trust in your partner's love, leading to a constant state of hypervigilance where you are always on the lookout for signs that they might leave.

These beliefs are not always conscious. They can sit quietly in the background of your mind, subtly influencing your behaviors, reactions, and emotional states. However, they powerfully shape your approach to relationships, often leaving you feeling insecure, anxious, and desperate for validation.

How These Beliefs Manifest in Relationships

These core beliefs often lead to behaviors rooted in fear rather than trust. You may find yourself overanalyzing every interaction with your partner, looking for signs that they might be pulling away. Simple things like a delayed response to a text message or a canceled date might trigger panic, leading you to question your partner's commitment. To prevent abandonment, you may go out of your way to please them, even sacrificing your own needs to maintain the connection.

This cycle can be exhausting, both for you and for your partner. The constant need for assurance can create a dynamic where your partner feels overwhelmed by your emotional demands, which may cause them to distance themselves—further fueling your anxiety. Over time, these patterns can erode the trust and intimacy in a relationship, making it difficult for either person to feel truly secure.

For example, if you believe that love must be earned, you might constantly seek ways to prove yourself in the relationship. You may take on more responsibilities, agree to things you don't truly want, or suppress your own needs to be seen as worthy of love. While this behavior may provide temporary encouragement, it often leads to feelings of resentment and burnout, as you realize that no amount of effort seems to truly alleviate your underlying fear of abandonment.

To provide a real-world example of how anxious attachment behaviors manifest in relationships, consider the case of Sarah and John from a couples therapy scenario. Sarah's anxious attachment style led her to frequently invade John's personal space and even go through his personal belongings. This behavior stemmed from Sarah's deep-seated fear of abandonment and a need for constant reassurance, typical of anxious attachment. John, on the other hand, felt violated by Sarah's actions, which eroded trust and created emotional distance between them. As Sarah's anxiety increased, she would alternate between being overly clingy and emotionally distant, which further destabilized their relationship(<u>Psychology Today</u>)(<u>Modern Wellness Counseling</u>).

This case illustrates how behaviors rooted in fear and insecurity can lead to tension, miscommunication, and an erosion of trust within relationships.

Challenging These Beliefs

The first step toward changing these patterns is to recognize and challenge the beliefs that underlie your anxious attachment. This process involves taking a closer look at where these beliefs came from and asking yourself whether they are truly serving you in your relationships.

Ask yourself the following questions:

1. **Where did this belief come from?**

Reflect on the origin of these beliefs. Were they instilled in you during childhood when your caregivers were emotionally distant or inconsistent? Did you learn that love was conditional, only given when you behaved in a certain way? Understanding the source of these beliefs can help you recognize that they are not facts—they are simply interpretations of past experiences.

2. **Is this belief based on reality, or is it something I learned from inconsistent caregiving?**

Challenge the validity of your beliefs. Ask yourself if it's really true that you must constantly prove your worth to be loved. Is it possible that this belief stems from the unpredictability of your early caregiving experiences rather than being an inherent truth about relationships? By questioning the basis of these beliefs, you begin to see them for what they are—learned responses, not objective reality.

3. Is this belief serving me?

Consider if these beliefs contribute to building healthy, secure relationships or if they keep you stuck in a cycle of anxiety and neediness. Anxious attachment beliefs often lead to behaviors that push people away rather than draw them closer. By recognizing that these beliefs no longer serve your best interests, you can start to let go of them and replace them with healthier, more empowering thoughts.

Rewriting Your Belief System

Once you've begun to challenge these beliefs, the next step is to actively replace them with new ones aligned with secure attachment. Instead of believing you are unworthy of love, remind yourself **you are enough** just as you are. You don't need to constantly prove your worth to be loved. Relationships are not about proving your value but are about mutual respect, care, and connection.

Consider adopting new beliefs such as:

- "I'm worthy of love and respect, exactly as I am."
- "I don't have to work for love; it is given freely in healthy relationships."
- "My value is inherent and does not depend on anyone else's approval."

As you begin to internalize these new beliefs, you'll notice a shift in how you approach relationships. Rather than feeling anxious and insecure, you'll start to feel more confident in your ability to connect with others in a healthy and balanced way. You'll no longer feel the need to constantly seek validation or fear that your partner will leave you. Instead, you'll trust in your own worth and in the strength of the connections you build.

Shaping Your Future with New Beliefs

Recognizing the impact of early bonds and challenging the beliefs that drive your anxious attachment is a critical step in your journey toward healing. These beliefs, formed in childhood, may have protected you in some ways at the time, but they are no longer serving you in your adult relationships. As you question and reframe these beliefs, you can begin to break free from anxious attachment patterns that have been holding you back. This will empower you to move toward a future where you feel secure, confident, and deeply connected in your relationships.

While this isn't an easy process, it's a transformative one. When you continue to reflect on your early bonds and challenge the beliefs you've carried with you, you're taking the first steps toward building a secure attachment that will allow you to thrive, both in your relationships and within yourself.

THE EMOTIONAL PATTERNS OF ANXIOUS ATTACHMENT

Anxious attachment can make relationships feel like a rollercoaster ride. There are moments of deep connection followed by overwhelming fear that the bond is in jeopardy. You may feel euphoric when your partner is attentive and affectionate, but devastated when they pull away, even if it's only temporary. This emotional back-and-forth is exhausting, not just for you but also for those you love.

The cycle often starts with small, seemingly insignificant triggers: a text that goes unanswered for a few hours, a change in your partner's tone of voice, or an unexpected cancellation of plans. These moments can send you into a spiral of anxious thoughts. You may start thinking, "What if they're mad at me?" or "What if they're losing interest?" This creates a constant feeling of being on edge, as if you're always waiting for the other shoe to drop.

THE NEED FOR REASSURANCE

At the core of anxious attachment is a profound need for reassurance. This need can be expressed in various ways—sometimes subtly, like frequently asking your partner if they love you or overanalyzing their words, texts, or gestures. At other times, it may take on more noticeable forms, such as becoming anxious when your partner doesn't respond to messages as quickly as you'd like or feeling panicked when there's a perceived distance between you.

The fear of abandonment often drives this need for reassurance. For someone with anxious attachment, love can feel uncertain and fragile, leading you to constantly question the authenticity of your partner's affection and whether it could vanish at any moment. This makes every interaction, no matter how small, seem like evidence of whether the relationship is stable or on the verge of crumbling.

Reassurance-seeking behaviors can range from asking for verbal affirmations of love ("Do you really love me?"), to checking in frequently with your partner for signs that the relationship is secure. This might mean constantly checking their mood, seeking validation through affection, or feeling compelled to clarify the status of your relationship. While occasional reassurance is a natural part of any relationship, for those with anxious attachment, this need becomes magnified to unhealthy levels, creating a cycle of anxiety and validation-seeking that can strain the relationship.

The problem lies in the fact that no amount of reassurance can provide lasting comfort. Even when your partner gives you the validation you crave, it often only soothes the anxiety temporarily. Soon after, doubts creep back in, leaving you once again needing confirmation that you are loved and valued. This relentless cycle can leave both you and your partner feeling drained, as the constant search for validation takes a toll on your emotional well-being and the relationship itself.

There were times in past relationships when I tended to seek a lot of reassurance from my partners. I'd ask them if they still loved me, if they were happy, and if they thought our relationship was okay. While their affirmations provided temporary relief, the underlying anxiety always returned, leaving me feeling like I was walking on eggshells.

HOW REASSURANCE-SEEKING CREATES A VICIOUS CYCLE

The paradox of anxious attachment is that seeking validation often leads to feeling less secure. Each attempt at reassurance temporarily eases anxiety but reinforces the belief that love and security must be constantly earned. You begin to rely more and more on external validation to feel okay, which further entrenches the anxious patterns that make you doubt the stability of your relationships.

For your partner, this dynamic can be equally exhausting. They may feel pressured to constantly provide reassurance, eventually leading to frustration or even withdrawal. If your partner has avoidant tendencies, this need for constant validation might push them away, amplifying the very fears you're trying to alleviate. This creates a self-fulfilling prophecy, where your need for reassurance drives your partner to distance themselves, and their distancing triggers even more anxiety and neediness on your part.

Over time, the relationship may feel more like a battlefield of emotional needs rather than a place of mutual support and trust. Recognizing how this pattern is fueled by your own internal fears and insecurities is crucial.

BREAKING THE CYCLE

Breaking free from the cycle of reassurance-seeking requires a fundamental shift in how you view yourself and your relationships. The first step to breaking this cycle is recognizing that your need for reassurance is rooted in anxious attachment, not necessarily your partner's actions. Once you acknowledge this, you can begin shifting your focus inward, working on developing internal security rather than relying on constant validation from others.

1. Building Internal Security

One of the most effective ways to reduce the need for external reassurance is by building **internal security**. This involves cultivating a stronger sense of self-worth and emotional independence so that your feelings of security are not entirely dependent on how others behave or respond to you. It may seem challenging at first, but learning how to feel secure within yourself without needing constant affirmation from your partner is possible.

59

Developing **self-validation** practices can help you break the cycle of reassurance-seeking. These practices involve learning how to give yourself the emotional support and reassurance you seek from others. By becoming your own source of validation, you can build emotional resilience, which makes you less likely to feel panicked or overwhelmed when your partner is unavailable or distant.

Here are some self-validation practices you can incorporate into your daily life:

- **Mindful Journaling** - Write down situations where you feel insecure and reflect on how you can manage those emotions internally. For example, if you feel anxious about your partner not responding to a text, journal about your feelings and remind yourself that your security isn't tied to their immediate response.

- **Create a Self-Validation Playlist** - Music can shift emotions quickly. Create a playlist of songs that make you feel empowered and independent. When you're feeling anxious or unsure, listen to this playlist to help you reconnect with your sense of self-worth.

- **Remember That Everyone Has Strengths and Weaknesses** - Instead of comparing yourself to others, remember that everyone has strengths and weaknesses. This helps you avoid placing others on a pedestal, which can diminish your own sense of value.

- **Invest Time in Personal Projects and Hobbies** - The more you invest in activities that bring you joy, the more you reinforce your self-worth. Pursuing hobbies you love or engaging in meaningful projects nurtures a sense of fulfillment that doesn't rely on external validation.

- **Focus on Self-Care** - Prioritizing self-care, such as setting boundaries, managing your workload, or ensuring you get enough rest, helps you treat yourself with the respect you deserve. Over time, caring for yourself improves self-esteem and reduces the need for external validation.

- **Notice How You Feel and What You Need** - Practice emotional awareness by acknowledging your feelings and understanding what you need in the moment. For example: "I feel anxious, and I need some quiet time to reflect."

- **Don't Over-Identify with Your Feelings** - Notice the difference between saying "I feel angry" and "I am angry." Acknowledge your emotions without letting them define you, reminding yourself that feelings are temporary and don't determine your worth.

- **Talk to Yourself Like a Friend** - Give yourself the kind of encouragement and affirmation you'd offer a close friend. For example, if you're feeling insecure, remind yourself, "I'm doing my best, and I'm proud of the progress I've made."

These practical strategies can help foster emotional independence and internal security, reducing the need for external reassurance and enhancing your overall well-being.

2. Recognizing and Addressing Triggers

Another important step in breaking this cycle is identifying your specific triggers. What situations or behaviors from your partner tend to spark your need for reassurance? Is it when they are busy and not texting you as frequently? Or maybe when they seem distracted or emotionally distant? Recognizing these triggers allows you to pause and reflect before reacting out of anxiety.

When a trigger arises, instead of immediately seeking validation from your partner, try to take a step back and remind yourself that your feelings of anxiety are rooted in your attachment style, not necessarily in the reality of the situation. You might tell yourself, "I'm feeling anxious because I'm afraid of being abandoned, but this doesn't mean my partner is actually going to leave me." By acknowledging the root of your anxiety, you can create space between the trigger and your emotional reaction, giving you more control over how you respond.

3. Reframing Your Internal Dialogue

Much of anxious attachment is fueled by negative self-talk—beliefs that you are not enough or that your partner will leave you if you don't constantly prove your worth. Reframing your internal dialogue and challenging these thoughts are necessary to break the cycle. Instead of thinking, "If I don't check in with them, they'll forget about me," try reframing it to, "I trust that my partner cares about me, even if they're not responding immediately."

Learning to trust in the security of the relationship—and more importantly, learning to trust yourself—is a crucial part of overcoming anxious attachment. Shifting your mindset from fear and insecurity to trust and confidence reduces the need for constant reassurance.

MOVING TOWARD AWARENESS AND HEALING

Breaking free from the emotional rollercoaster of anxious attachment takes time, patience, and self-awareness. When you recognize your need for validation is rooted in your attachment style, not in the reality of your relationship, you can begin to shift the focus inward and cultivate a sense of internal security. Building emotional independence and learning to validate yourself are critical steps on this journey.

The emotional highs and lows of anxious attachment may feel overwhelming, but they are not permanent.

Understanding the brain's role in triggering responses and learning to regulate emotions can help break free from anxious cycles and insecurity.

As you continue on this journey, remember that your brain's capacity for change is limitless. You have the power to reshape your attachment patterns and build the secure, fulfilling relationships you deserve. In the next chapter, we'll delve deeper into identifying and managing the triggers that activate your attachment anxiety, empowering you to take back control of your emotional well-being.

CHAPTER 2: IDENTIFYING YOUR ANXIOUS TRIGGERS

One of the first steps in overcoming anxious attachment is learning to recognize the triggers that activate your anxiety. These triggers often appear as subtle cues—unanswered messages, shifts in tone, or changes in routine—that leave you feeling uncertain, panicked, or even abandoned.

The good news is that by identifying and understanding these triggers, you can take steps to reduce their impact on your relationships and emotional well-being. In this chapter, we'll explore the most common anxious attachment triggers, help you

67

understand how these triggers manifest in your behavior, and provide tools for tracking and managing them over time.

WHAT TRIGGERS ANXIOUS ATTACHMENT?

Triggers are emotional landmines that set off your attachment anxiety. These disruptions don't have to be large or overt; even small changes in your partner's behavior or communication can trigger deep-seated fears of rejection or abandonment.

Here are some of the most common triggers for anxious attachment:

1. Inconsisent Communication

When your partner doesn't respond to messages as quickly as you'd like, or when communication feels inconsistent, it can spark a feeling of abandonment. Even something as simple as a delayed reply can be enough to send you spiraling into worry.

2. Perceived Distance

If your partner seems emotionally distant—whether they're distracted by work, stress, or personal issues— it can trigger fears that they are pulling away or losing interest. The fear that your relationship is at risk can lead to heightened anxiety and clingy behavior.

3. Perceived Changes in Affection

When affection levels fluctuate, you may find yourself panicking. For instance, if your partner isn't being as physically or verbally affectionate as they once were, your mind might spiral. You might wonder whether they're pulling away, losing interest, or on the verge of ending the relationship. These fears are often based on perception rather than reality, but they feel incredibly real in the moment.

4. Unmet Expectations

Expectations play a significant role in relationships, especially when it comes to anxious attachment. If your partner cancels plans, forgets something important, or fails to meet your emotional needs, you might interpret it as a sign that they no longer care.

These unmet expectations can leave you feeling hurt, rejected, or insecure.

5. Conflict or Disagreement

Conflict is a natural part of any relationship, but for someone with anxious attachment, even small disagreements can trigger overwhelming fear. If you feel like the conflict hasn't been resolved or that your partner is upset, it can lead to intense worry that the relationship is falling apart. Conflict may trigger fears of abandonment or rejection, causing you to question if your partner is still committed to the relationship.

As discussed in the last chapter, you'll want to keep in mind that these triggers often stem from your attachment history, not necessarily from the reality of your current relationship. Your brain is wired to perceive emotional distance as a threat based on past experiences of inconsistency or neglect. By understanding this, you can separate past fears from present realities.

HOW ANXIETY MANIFESTS IN RELATIONSHIPS

Anxious attachment can manifest in various ways, shaping how you communicate, behave, and emotionally react to your partner. Below are some common behaviors driven by the need to restore a sense of closeness and security, often with unintended consequences.

1. Overthinking and Overanalyzing

One of the most common manifestations of anxious attachment is overthinking. You might find yourself analyzing every word, gesture, or text message from your partner, trying to decode whether they're upset, distant, or losing interest. This constant mental analysis creates a cycle of anxiety, where you look for signs that something is wrong, even when everything might be fine.

I remember a time when my partner was engrossed in a work project, and her lack of frequent communication sent me into a tailspin. I spent hours dissecting our past conversations, convinced she was pulling away. In reality, she was just focused on her work, but my anxiety made me interpret her behavior as a threat to our relationship.

2. Validation-Seeking

When triggered, you may seek reassurance from your partner by asking them whether they still love you, whether they're upset, or if everything is okay. While it's normal to seek reassurance in any relationship, excessive reassurance-seeking can become a problem when it's driven by fear rather than genuine communication. Over time, this behavior can put a strain on the relationship, as your partner may feel overwhelmed by the constant need to reassure.

3. Emotional Outbursts

Intense feelings triggered by anxious attachment can sometimes lead to emotional outbursts. You might become upset or angry if your partner doesn't meet your expectations or if you feel rejected. These emotional reactions derive from fear, but they can come across as accusations or criticism, making it difficult to resolve the underlying issue.

I vividly recall one particular evening when my partner and I were supposed to spend time together. She'd had a long day at work, and while I was eagerly anticipating our time, she seemed distracted and distant. We sat on the couch, and I kept glancing over at her, expecting her to engage in conversation or at least ask about my day. Instead, she was scrolling through her phone, absorbed in something else. My mind instantly began to race. *Why isn't she paying attention to me? Is something wrong? Is she upset with me?*

The more she stayed quiet, the more my anxiety built. I could feel the tightness in my chest, and before I knew it, I blurted out, "Are you even listening to me? Or would you rather be anywhere else right now?" My tone was sharp, my words a reflection of the growing panic inside me. But in reality, I wasn't angry—I was scared. Scared that her lack of attention meant something was wrong between us.

She looked up, surprised and confused, not knowing where this sudden accusation had come from. She calmly tried to explain that she was just unwinding after a stressful day, but I couldn't hear her reasoning over my own spiraling thoughts. The conversation quickly escalated into an argument, with me doubling down on my frustrations, even though deep down, all I wanted was reassurance and closeness.

Looking back, I realized that my emotional outburst—rooted in insecurity—pushed her further away, the exact opposite of what I needed. The more I lashed out, the more distant she became, which only made me feel more abandoned. It was a painful cycle, driven by my inability to manage my own anxiety in the moment.

4. Clinging or Desperation

In moments of intense anxiety, you might feel a desperate need to be close to your partner—both emotionally and physically. You may find yourself clinging to them, wanting constant contact or confirmation that they won't leave. While seeking closeness is a natural part of relationships, anxious attachment can cause this behavior to become excessive, leading to feelings of suffocation or emotional exhaustion for you and your partner.

IDENTIFYING AND TRACKING YOUR TRIGGERS

Now that we understand how anxious attachment can appear in your behaviors, let's move into the practical work of identifying your unique triggers. Understanding your anxious triggers is the first step toward managing them. To gain control over your emotional responses, it's helpful to track your triggers over time. Keeping a record of what situations or behaviors trigger your anxiety will help you respond more effectively.

Exercise: Identifying and Tracking Triggers

Create a log of your anxious triggers over the next week. Write down the following details whenever you feel your anxiety spike:

1. The Situation: Describe what happened in the moment you felt anxious. Was it a lack of communication? Did your partner seem distant or distracted?

2. Your Emotional Reaction: How did you feel in response to this trigger? Were you scared, angry, sad, or overwhelmed? Rate the intensity of your emotion on a scale of 1-10.

3. Your Physical Reaction: Did you notice any physical symptoms of anxiety, such as a racing heart, sweating, or restlessness?

4. Your Behavioral Response: How did you respond to the trigger? Did you reach out to your partner for reassurance? Did you overthink the situation or become upset?

After a week, review your log. Look for recurring patterns or situations that consistently trigger your anxiety. Becoming aware of these patterns is vital to breaking free from the cycle of anxious attachment.

REFRAMING YOUR TRIGGERS

Another powerful tool for gaining control over your triggers is reframing. The process of reframing triggers starts with recognizing that many of your emotional reactions are tied to past experiences rather than the present reality. By shifting your focus from fear to curiosity, you can question the automatic thoughts and assumptions that drive your anxiety. For example, instead of assuming that your partner's sudden quietness during a conversation means they're angry or upset, consider other possibilities—maybe they're tired or deep in thought about something unrelated to the relationship. This shift in thinking reduces the power of the trigger, helping you respond more thoughtfully.

To reframe your triggers, ask yourself:

- Is this fear based on fact, or is it an assumption?

  Challenge your automatic thoughts and consider alternative explanations for the situation.

  - For example, if your partner hasn't texted you back in a few hours, rather than assuming they're upset or losing interest, consider other explanations. They might be busy, their phone could be on silent, or they might simply need some alone time.

- What other possible interpretations exist for this situation?

  Explore other possible interpretations of the situation. Remember, anxious attachment can sometimes lead us to jump to negative conclusions. You can diffuse your anxiety by considering alternative perspectives.

- What can I do to address this trigger in a healthy way?

  Instead of reacting impulsively, think about what you need in the moment. Do you need to communicate with your partner about how you're feeling? Or would it be more helpful to practice self-soothing techniques and give yourself the reassurance you're seeking?

Over time, this practice not only helps you break the cycle of overthinking but also begins to rewire your brain's automatic responses to emotional uncertainty. The more you challenge your anxious thoughts, the stronger the new neural pathways in your brain become, leading to a more secure and stable emotional response in the long term.

THE ROLE OF OVERTHINKING IN ANXIOUS ATTACHMENT

While reframing triggers is essential, those with anxious attachment often struggle with overthinking. Let's explore how overthinking can fuel anxiety and ways to escape this pattern.

For individuals with anxious attachment, overthinking becomes a default response to emotional uncertainty. Overthinking often begins when something triggers your anxiety, such as when your partner doesn't text back, or they seem less affectionate than usual. Your brain leaps into action, analyzing every detail of your interactions in an attempt to "solve" the perceived problem.

But instead of finding clarity, overthinking tends to magnify your anxiety. You replay conversations in your mind, searching for hidden meanings or signs that something is wrong. You might question if your partner's tone was off, if they were paying enough attention to you, or if they seemed distant. As your thoughts spiral, you convince yourself that there's a deeper problem at hand, even if there's no concrete evidence to support this fear.

WHY OVERTHINKING HAPPENS

Overthinking is primarily driven by a desire for **certainty**. When you're uncertain about how your partner feels, your mind goes into overdrive, trying to scrutinize and interpret every possible outcome. It's almost as if you believe that by excessively analyzing the situation, you can prevent the worst from happening—whether that's a breakup, a conflict, or emotional distance.

In a relationship context, overthinking can manifest like:

- Constantly replaying conversations in your head, trying to interpret every word or tone your partner used.
- Spending hours thinking about what your partner really meant when they said something.
- Trying to determine whether their actions are signs of commitment or disinterest.

This relentless need for certainty is rooted in a deep-seated fear of abandonment. Your brain, in its attempt to shield you from emotional pain, goes into overdrive, trying to anticipate and control every possible outcome. However, this mental hypervigilance rarely leads to the clarity you seek. Instead, it intensifies your anxiety, fostering doubt in your partner's intentions and making you hyperfocused on imagined threats, even when there's no evidence to support them.

Overthinking rarely provides answers. Instead, it feeds your anxiety and keeps you stuck in a cycle of doubt and insecurity. This mental

81

hypervigilance not only drains your energy but also affects your partner, who may feel overwhelmed by your constant need for reassurance.

This cycle of overthinking creates **emotional distance** in relationships. It often results in you feeling less secure despite the very real efforts your partner may be making to reassure you. In many cases, your partner may be unaware of the storm of thoughts going on in your mind, which can further exacerbate feelings of isolation and insecurity.

Now that you've gained insight into the roots of overthinking, let's examine how to liberate ourselves from this cycle and cultivate a calmer mind.

BREAKING THE OVERTHINKING CYCLE

Breaking free from overthinking requires conscious effort and practice. Here are some vital strategies to help you regain control over your emotional responses.

1. Recognize When You're Overthinking

The first step to overcoming overthinking is **awareness**. Begin by noticing when you start to ruminate or spiral into endless analysis of your partner's actions or words. Pay attention to physical or emotional cues that signal you're starting to overthink, like tightness in your chest, racing thoughts, or an overwhelming urge to "figure out" what's going on. Once you recognize that you're falling into an overthinking pattern, you can take steps to redirect your focus.

By catching yourself in the act, you can remind yourself that this is a **mental habit** tied to anxious attachment, and it doesn't reflect the reality of your relationship.

2. Challenge Your Thoughts

The next time you catch yourself overanalyzing, ask yourself these questions:

- **Is there evidence to support my fears?**

Overthinking is often based on assumptions rather than facts. Pause and ask yourself if there is any concrete evidence that your partner is upset, distant, or withdrawing. If there isn't, your anxiety is likely creating a false narrative.

For instance, consider Jane and Mark. Jane was quick to jump to conclusions when Mark canceled their dinner plans last minute. She immediately thought, "He must be upset with me," or, "He's losing interest." However, when Jane paused to evaluate the situation more objectively, she realized that Mark had been under a lot of pressure at work, and there was no real evidence that he was upset with her. By focusing on the actual facts instead of assumptions, Jane was able to calm her anxiety and approach the situation with more clarity, ultimately preventing unnecessary conflict.

- **What's the worst that could happen?**

Overthinking is often driven by a fear of worst-case scenarios. But instead of letting that fear control your thoughts, try to confront it head-on. Ask yourself: "What's the worst that could happen?" and then assess whether it's truly catastrophic. Most of the time, the worst-case scenario is far less likely or damaging than you might think. By acknowledging it, you can reduce its hold over you and focus on more realistic outcomes.

- **How can I communicate instead of ruminate?**

Overthinking thrives in the absence of communication. Rather than letting your thoughts get out of control, consider talking to your partner. If something is bothering you, ask for **clarification** or **reassurance** in a healthy, direct way. This can provide the clarity you need and prevent you from ruminating on what might be nothing more than a misunderstanding. For example, instead of overanalyzing why your partner hasn't responded to the text message you sent hours ago when they return home from work, you can calmly ask, "Hey, is everything okay? I noticed you've been quiet today." This simple question can prevent hours of overthinking and provide immediate relief.

Breaking free from overthinking isn't just about

stopping a behavior—it's about **rewiring** your thought patterns and building new, healthier ways of responding to emotional uncertainty.

Here are a few practices that can help you retrain your brain and reduce the hold that overthinking has on your relationships:

1. **Set a Time Limit for Rumination:** If you find yourself stuck in a loop of anxious thoughts, give yourself a set amount of time—say, 10 minutes—to think about the issue. After that, distract yourself with a different activity, such as reading, exercising, or talking to a friend.

2. **Ground Yourself in the Present Moment:** Overthinking often pulls you into a future filled with worst-case scenarios. Ground yourself by focusing on what's happening right now—not what might happen later. Practice mindfulness exercises, like deep breathing or focusing

on your surroundings, to bring your attention back to the present.

3. **Reality-Check Your Assumptions:** When your mind jumps to conclusions, challenge those assumptions. For example, if you think, "They didn't respond because they're losing interest," ask yourself, "Is there another reason they might be busy? Have they done this before, and everything was fine?"

4. **Mindfulness and Grounding Techniques:** Mindfulness is a powerful tool for managing overthinking. When you find yourself ruminating, practicing mindfulness can help bring you back to the present moment. Try focusing on your breath, noticing the sensations in your body, or engaging in a grounding exercise like counting the objects around you. These practices can shift your attention away from anxious thoughts and help you feel more centered.

5. **Cognitive Restructuring:** Cognitive restructuring is a technique from cognitive-behavioral therapy (CBT) that involves identifying and challenging negative or distorted thoughts. When you notice yourself overthinking, write down the thoughts that are running through your mind. Challenge each one by asking, "Is this thought true?" or "Is there another way to look at this?" This process helps you question the validity of your anxious thoughts and replace them with more balanced perspectives.

6. **Trust-Building Practices:** Overthinking often stems from a lack of trust—both in yourself and in your partner. To reduce overthinking, work on building trust in your relationships. This might involve small steps, like acknowledging when your partner follows through on promises or expressing gratitude for the ways they show up for you. Over time, these

trust-building practices can help reduce the need for constant analysis and help you feel more secure in your relationship.

GAINING CONTROL OVER YOUR TRIGGERS

Understanding your anxious triggers is empowering. It allows you to recognize when your brain's alarm system is activated, flooding your body with stress hormones in response to a perceived threat. The key is that you can retrain your brain. By consciously addressing these triggers, you can cultivate calmer, more controlled responses.

Once you become aware of these triggers, you can take steps to prevent overthinking from spiraling out of control. For example, when you recognize a trigger (like a delayed text or a distant partner), rather than immediately jumping to worst-case scenarios, you can take a breath, assess the situation more calmly, and remind yourself that this reaction is rooted in past experiences. This pause allows the prefrontal cortex—

the part of your brain responsible for rational thinking—to regain control, reducing the emotional intensity and giving you more clarity.

Over time, this practice will help you build a more secure attachment style, where you can trust both yourself and your partner without the constant fear of abandonment. Take responsibility for your emotional responses to reclaim your power and open the door to deeper, more fulfilling relationships.

In the next chapter, we'll focus on shifting your mindset from anxious to secure. You'll learn how to rewrite your internal dialogue, challenge limiting beliefs, and cultivate a healthier, more confident approach to relationships. By the end of this book, you'll have established the foundation for a life characterized by emotional security and healthy connections.

CHAPTER 3: SHIFTING YOUR MINDSET

If you've lived with anxious attachment for most of your life, it can feel as though your thoughts and emotions are wired to expect the worst in relationships. Shifting from an anxious attachment style to a more secure way of thinking requires a deep, internal transformation of your mindset.

Anxious attachment can make you feel trapped in cycles of doubt, fear, and insecurity. However, by actively working to change your thoughts and beliefs, you can begin to build the internal security necessary for healthier, more stable relationships. This chapter will cover methods for shifting from an anxious to a

93

secure mindset by rewriting your internal dialogue, reframing reassurance-seeking behavior, challenging limiting beliefs, and using practical mindset exercises to help you find emotional balance and confidence.

REWRITING YOUR INTERNAL DIALOGUE

One of the most powerful tools in overcoming anxious attachment is changing the way you talk to yourself. Your internal dialogue—the running commentary inside your mind—shapes how you view yourself, others, and relationships. For those with anxious attachment, this dialogue is often filled with fear, self-doubt, and negative assumptions, such as:

- "I'm not enough."
- "They're going to leave me."
- "They don't love me as much as I love them."
- "If they cared, they would reassure me more."

These beliefs may seem real, but the truth is they're no. These thoughts are not based on facts but fear-driven narratives that you've internalized from past experiences. They are old patterns designed to protect you from the pain of rejection or abandonment. But these patterns are now outdated, and rather than protecting you, they are keeping you stuck in the very thing you're trying to avoid—emotional instability and insecurity.

The good news is that you can rewrite this internal dialogue. It starts with recognizing when those fear-driven thoughts arise and challenging them with more balanced, reality-based alternatives. Instead of jumping to the conclusion and telling yourself, "They're going to leave me," you could try thinking, "This is just my anxiety speaking; there's no evidence that they are pulling away." This doesn't mean ignoring your feelings but acknowledging the difference between fear-based thinking and actual facts.

WHY YOUR INTERNAL DIALOGUE MATTERS

Your internal dialogue is more powerful than you might realize. It shapes not only how you feel about yourself but also how you interact with others. If you constantly tell yourself that you're unlovable or your partner is on the verge of leaving, those thoughts will influence your behavior. You may become overly needy, cling to your partner for reassurance, or interpret neutral situations as signs of rejection. Over time, this creates a self-fulfilling prophecy where your anxious behaviors push your partner away, confirming the very fears you were trying to avoid.

The way you speak to yourself profoundly impacts your emotions and actions. Research shows that your brain tends to respond to your thoughts as though they are facts, regardless of their accuracy. This concept is rooted in cognitive behavioral science, where the brain's tendency to interpret repeated thoughts as reality can trigger corresponding emotional and physiological reactions. For example, when your internal dialogue is filled with self-doubt and fear of abandonment, your brain responds by activating stress responses, reinforcing those negative feelings, and potentially influencing behaviors that push your partner away. Neuroscientific studies, like those on neuroplasticity, demonstrate that consistent patterns of negative thinking strengthen neural pathways associated with fear and anxiety. However, by consciously shifting to more positive and supportive affirmations, you can rewire your brain, creating new pathways that foster emotional resilience, security, and self-worth in your relationships.

The goal isn't to ignore or suppress your anxious thoughts but to **challenge and reframe them**. By learning to recognize when your internal dialogue is driven by fear and replacing those thoughts with more compassionate, balanced beliefs, you can break the cycle of anxious attachment.

Let's take a closer look at the specific negative narratives that often fuel anxious attachment.

RECOGNIZING THE NEGATIVE NARRATIVES

The first step in rewriting your internal dialogue is becoming aware of the negative narratives that dominate your thinking. These are the automatic thoughts that surface when you feel uncertain, insecure, or anxious in your relationships. For many people with anxious attachment, these thoughts are deeply ingrained, often rooted in childhood experiences where love and validation were inconsistent.

Common anxious attachment narratives include:

- **"If they don't respond right away, they're pulling away from me."**

  This thought reflects a fear of abandonment, where any perceived distance from your partner is interpreted as a sign that they're losing interest or preparing to leave.

- **"I have to work hard to be loved."**

This belief often stems from a history of conditional love in which someone was only shown affection when they met certain expectations. It can lead to overcompensation in relationships, where you feel the need to constantly prove your worth to avoid being abandoned.

- **"They'll leave me once they realize who I really am."**

This reflects a deep fear of being unworthy of love, where you believe that if your partner truly knew you, they would no longer want to be with you. This thought drives behaviors like hiding your true feelings, avoiding conflict, or becoming overly accommodating to keep your partner happy.

Recognizing these narratives is crucial because they are not facts—they are interpretations based on fear. By identifying them, you can begin the process of questioning and rewriting them.

How Negative Self-Talk Sabotages Your Relationships

When your internal dialogue is dominated by negative self-talk, it's easy to spiral into a cycle of fear and insecurity. You might start to interpret every action (or inaction) from your partner as a sign that something is wrong in the relationship. A delayed response, a missed call, or a busy day can quickly turn into thoughts like, "They're losing interest," or "They don't care about me anymore."

This type of thinking not only increases your anxiety but also affects the way you communicate with your partner. You might become more clingy, demanding, or emotionally reactive, unintentionally pushing your partner away and reinforcing your fears.

Now that we've reviewed the detrimental impact of negative self-talk, let's go over actionable steps to rewrite your internal dialogue and foster a more positive and empowering mindset.

STEPS TO REWRITING YOUR INTERNAL DIALOGUE

1. Identify Your Negative Thoughts: The first step to rewriting your internal dialogue is to become aware of the negative thoughts that pop up when you feel anxious or insecure. Write down these thoughts so you can examine them more clearly.

   Example: "If they don't reply soon, it means they don't care about me anymore."

2. Challenge the Thought: Once you've identified a negative thought, ask yourself whether it's based on facts or assumptions. Is there concrete evidence to support this fear, or is it just your anxiety speaking? Many times, you'll

find that these thoughts are fueled by fear rather than reality.

Example: "Is it really true that a delayed reply means they don't care? Could it be that they're busy or preoccupied?"

3. Replace with a Balanced Thought: After challenging the negative thought, replace it with a more balanced, realistic perspective. This new thought should focus on facts and logic, rather than fear and assumptions.

Example: "A delayed reply doesn't mean they don't care. They've been consistent in showing affection, and it's normal for someone to be busy or take time to respond."

4. Practice Self-Compassion: Be kind to yourself as you go through this process. It's natural to have negative thoughts, especially if anxious attachment has been part of your life for a long time. Remind yourself that you are learning and growing, and that change takes time.

5. **Practice Gratitude**: Regularly practicing gratitude helps shift your focus from what is lacking or feared to what is already present and fulfilling in your life. This habit helps rewire your brain to notice the positives more frequently, reducing anxiety. Take a moment to reflect on the aspects of your relationship or your personal life that make you feel loved and secure.

Shifting your mindset, rewriting your internal dialogue, and challenging negative thoughts are crucial steps in breaking free from the cycle of anxiety and insecurity. By learning how to challenge negative self-talk and replace it with empowering beliefs, you gain control over your emotional responses. For more strategies on transforming your mindset and mastering your thoughts, I recommend reading my bestseller *"How to Stop Being Negative, Angry, and Mean: Master Your Mind and Take Control of Your Life,"* which provides actionable techniques to help you take charge of your mental well-being.

Beyond transforming your internal dialogue, it's equally important to address the external behaviors that often accompany anxious attachment, such as the constant need for reassurance. Let's explore how to reframe this need and develop healthier ways to seek validation.

REFRAMING REASSURANCE SEEKING

One characteristic of anxious attachment involves the need for constant reassurance. Whether it's asking your partner if they love you or seeking validation through texts and affection, reassurance-seeking becomes a way to soothe the fear of abandonment or rejection. However, this behavior can often backfire, straining your relationship and reinforcing the very insecurities you're trying to overcome.

Reframing how you seek reassurance can be a game-changer in your relationships. Keep in mind that this isn't about suppressing your need for reassurance. Instead, you're learning how to ask for it in a healthy, balanced way.

Healthy Ways to Seek Reassurance

1. Be Direct and Specific: Instead of asking vague or repetitive questions like, "Do you still love me?" or "Are you mad at me?", be specific about what you need in the moment. For example, you could say, "I'm feeling a bit anxious today. Can we talk for a few minutes so I can feel more connected?"

2. Acknowledge Your Insecurities: Let your partner know that you're working on managing your attachment anxiety, but there may be times when you still need reassurance. This will encourage an open discussion without making your partner feel responsible for constantly alleviating your fears.

3. Balance Reassurance with Self-Soothing: When you feel the urge to ask for reassurance, pause and try to comfort yourself first. Use grounding techniques or remind yourself of the positive aspects of your relationship before reaching out for validation. This helps reduce dependency on external validation and builds emotional resilience.

I used to constantly ask my partner, "Do you still love me?" seeking reassurance whenever anxiety crept in. Over time, I realized this wasn't fostering a true connection. Instead, I learned to express my needs more directly. For instance, if I felt insecure after a disagreement, I'd say, "I'm still feeling a little unsettled from our conversation earlier. Can we talk about it more?' This shift towards open communication not only addressed my needs but also deepened our intimacy.

Now, let's explore some common limiting beliefs that contribute to anxious attachment and how to challenge them.

CHALLENGING LIMITING BELIEFS

Let's talk about the limiting beliefs that fuel anxious attachment. Limiting beliefs are deep-rooted convictions that hold you back from forming secure, fulfilling relationships. They are often subconscious, ingrained from childhood or past relationships, and can sound like:

-

  "I'm not worthy of love."
- "If I don't constantly prove myself, they'll lose interest."
- "Love is conditional; I have to work for it."

These beliefs are at the heart of anxious attachment because they distort how you interpret your partner's actions. When you believe, "I'm not enough," every time your partner seems distant, your brain will automatically jump to the conclusion that they're losing interest. You may not even question this thought—it feels like the truth because you've lived with this belief for so long.

The crucial realization is that these limiting beliefs are not truths; they're perceptions shaped by past experiences. For years, I carried the belief that "I won't find someone who will truly love me." This stemmed from childhood experiences where affection felt conditional. But through research and self-reflection, I learned to challenge this belief. I started asking myself, "Is there evidence in my life that contradicts this belief?" and "What would happen if I chose to believe I am capable of finding and experiencing true love?" Gradually, I began to rewrite this narrative, and it transformed my relationships.

To challenge limiting beliefs, start by asking yourself:

1. **Where did this belief come from?** Was it something you learned from your early caregivers? Did you feel like love was only given when you acted a certain way?

2. **Is this belief serving me now?** Does thinking, "I have to earn love," help you feel secure, or does it keep you stuck in fear and insecurity?

3. **Is this belief grounded on reality, or is it a narrative I've been telling myself?** If you constantly feel like you have to prove your worth, ask yourself,

"What would happen if I just trusted that I am enough as I am?"

In addition to challenging limiting beliefs, actively practicing new ways of thinking can accelerate your journey toward secure attachment. Here are some mindset exercises to help you reinforce a more secure and confident outlook.

MINDSET EXERCISES

Changing your mindset from anxious to secure takes time and intentional effort. Below are some exercises you can use to reinforce a more secure mindset in your daily life:

1. Daily Affirmations

Affirmations are statements of intention that you repeat to yourself regularly to rewire your brain and cultivate a more secure mindset. Here are a few affirmations that can help you rewrite your internal dialogue:

- "I am deserving of love and connection."
- "I trust myself to navigate relationships with confidence and security."
- "My worth is not defined by how others treat me."
- "I can handle challenges in relationships with grace and resilience."

By repeating these affirmations daily, you begin to internalize these new beliefs, gradually replacing the negative narratives that have fueled your anxious attachment.

2. Visualization

Spend a few minutes each day visualizing yourself as securely attached. Imagine how you would feel in a relationship where you trust your partner, communicate openly, and don't fear abandonment. Focus on the emotions you would experience—peace, confidence, and stability.

3. Gratitude Journaling

At the end of each day, write down three things you're grateful for in your relationship or your life. This helps shift your focus from what's missing or wrong to what's going well, fostering a more secure mindset.

A NEW WAY OF THINKING

One of the crucial transitions in moving from anxious to secure attachment is learning to trust— both in yourself and in your relationships. For someone with anxious attachment, trust can feel elusive, especially when you're used to relying on external validation to feel secure. But trust isn't just something you give to others; it's something you cultivate within yourself.

To develop secure attachment, you need to shift from a mindset of fear and scarcity ("I'm afraid they'll leave," "I'm not enough") to a mindset of trust and abundance ("I trust that I am enough," "I trust that my partner cares for me"). This mindset shift doesn't happen overnight, but with practice, you can build a strong foundation of trust in your relationships.

Here are some key actions to shift from fear to trust:

1. **Challenge the Assumptions Behind Your Fears**: When fear arises, ask yourself, "Is this fear rooted in fact, or is it an assumption?" If your partner hasn't texted back, instead of assuming they're pulling away, remind yourself that there could be a variety of reasons—none of which have to do with their feelings for you.

2. **Practice Trust in Small Steps**: Building trust takes time, so start small. If you're used to constantly seeking reassurance, try waiting an extra hour before asking for it. This small change will help you develop internal resilience and reinforce that you don't need constant validation to feel secure.

3. **Build Self-Trust**: The most important trust you can build is with yourself. Trust that you are enough and capable of handling whatever comes your way. Your worth is not dependent on someone else's validation.

Shifting from fear to trust involves rewiring your brain to respond differently to emotional triggers, going beyond simply changing your mindset. Each time you practice trusting yourself and your relationships, you're strengthening new neural pathways that reinforce security, rather than fear.

In the following chapter, we'll dive into developing emotional self-regulation, a critical tool for managing anxiety, especially when anxious triggers arise. You'll learn how to calm emotional storms and find stability even in the most challenging moments, paving the way for emotional independence and freedom.

CHAPTER 4: DEVELOPING EMOTIONAL SELF-REGULATION

Emotional self-regulation is the ability to manage your emotional responses in a healthy, balanced way. Individuals with anxious attachment may find it especially challenging to manage their emotions. Experiencing triggers—whether it's a perceived distance from your partner, a delay in communication, or a moment of conflict—can cause overwhelming emotions, like anxiety, to spiral out of control. During these moments, it may feel like your emotions are in control, dictating your actions and reactions.

However, learning to regulate your emotions is not only possible but crucial for breaking the cycle of anxious attachment. Emotional self-regulation helps you create a pause between your feelings and your reactions, allowing you to respond in ways that are thoughtful, intentional, and aligned with your values rather than fear or insecurity. The focus of this chapter is to guide you in developing emotional self-regulation, offering practical techniques to effectively manage anxiety and strengthen emotional resilience over time.

UNDERSTANDING EMOTIONAL FLOODING

Emotional flooding occurs when your emotions become so intense that they overwhelm your ability to think clearly and respond rationally. For those with anxious attachment, emotional flooding is a frequent experience. It's that feeling of being completely consumed by fear, jealousy, or worry, which can be triggered by something as simple as a delayed text or a partner seeming distant.

I remember one evening when a past partner mentioned she was going out with friends after work. My mind immediately started racing. What if she meets someone else? What if she has more fun without me? These thoughts escalated quickly, and soon, I was gripped by a sense of panic. My heart pounded, my breathing became shallow, and I couldn't focus on anything else.

When emotional flooding happens, your body activates the **sympathetic nervous system**, preparing you for a "fight, flight, or freeze" response. This physiological reaction is an automatic survival mechanism designed to protect you from danger. But when you have anxious attachment, your brain often interprets emotional uncertainty as a threat, causing the same kind of physical and emotional reaction that you would experience in a truly dangerous situation.

Signs of emotional flooding include:

- Racing thoughts that spiral out of control.
- Difficulty breathing or a tight feeling in the chest.
- A strong urge to act impulsively (e.g., sending multiple texts, confronting your partner).
- Feeling trapped in overwhelming emotions, such as anger, fear, or jealousy.

Understanding that emotional flooding is a **physiological** reaction can help you take the steps needed to calm yourself during these moments. Your brain and body are reacting as if they're in danger, but in reality, the danger is perceived rather than real.

CALMING THE STORM: SELF-REGULATION TECHNIQUES

When emotional flooding occurs, it's important to have techniques ready to calm your nervous system and return to a state of balance. Here are some key strategies that can help you manage overwhelming emotions and regain control of the moment:

1. Grounding Exercises

Grounding exercises are simple, physical techniques that help bring your focus away from your anxiety and back into the present moment. When those moments of panic strike, I've personally found the 5-4-3-2-1 technique to be incredibly helpful. By focusing on my senses—the feel of the cool tile beneath my feet, the sound of the birds chirping outside, the taste of a mint tea—I'm able to anchor myself in the present and create a sense of calm amidst the emotional storm.

Grounding Exercise: 5-4-3-2-1 Technique

- 5: Look around and identify five things you can see.
- 4: Identify four things you can touch. Focus on the textures or sensations.
- 3: Identify three things you can hear in your environment.

- 2: Identify two things you can smell (or imagine two scents you enjoy).
- 1: Identify one thing you can taste or a taste you like (such as mint or chocolate).

This exercise helps shift your focus from your anxious thoughts to your physical senses, helping you calm down.

2. Deep Breathing

When you're in the midst of anxiety, your breathing often becomes shallow and rapid, which signals to your body that you're in danger. By practicing deep, slow breathing, you can send signals to your brain that you are safe, which helps deactivate the fight-or-flight response.

How to Practice Deep Breathing:

- Sit or stand in a comfortable position.
- Inhale slowly through your nose for a count of four, filling your lungs.
- Hold your breath for a count of four.

- Exhale slowly through your mouth for a count of six.
- Repeat this process for several minutes until you feel your body start to relax.

Deep breathing activates the parasympathetic nervous system, which is responsible for calming your body down after stress.

3. Progressive Muscle Relaxation

Anxiety often causes tension in the body, especially in the neck, shoulders, and jaw. Progressive muscle relaxation is a technique that involves tensing and then relaxing each muscle group in your body, helping you release physical tension and calm your mind.

How to Practice Progressive Muscle Relaxation:

- Find a quiet space where you can sit or lie down comfortably.
- Start with your toes, curling them tightly for a count of five, then releasing.

- Move up to your legs, squeezing the muscles in your calves and thighs for five seconds, then releasing.
- Continue this process with each muscle group, working your way up through your torso, arms, and face.
- As you release each muscle, focus on the sensation of relaxation and let your body sink deeper into a state of calm.

4. Mindfulness and Meditation

Mindfulness is the practice of staying present with your thoughts and emotions without judgment. It allows you to observe your anxiety without getting caught up in it, which can help prevent emotional flooding from taking over.

- **Mindful Observation**: Take a few moments to observe your thoughts without trying to change or control them. Imagine them as clouds passing through the sky— temporary and non-threatening.

- **Body Scan Meditation**: Focus on each part of your body, starting from your toes and moving upward. Notice any tension or discomfort. This practice helps ground you in your physical sensations rather than your racing thoughts.

5. Learning to Pause Before Reacting

One of the most challenging aspects of managing anxious attachment is resisting the urge to react impulsively to emotional triggers. When anxiety strikes, your first instinct may be to reach out to your partner for reassurance, confront them about perceived distance, or immediately try to fix the situation. However, giving in to these impulses often leads to regret and can further strain the relationship.

Creating a Pause between your trigger and your response gives you time to regulate your emotions and choose a more thoughtful, intentional action.

How to Create a Pause:

1. Notice the Trigger: The first step is to recognize when you've been triggered. You might feel your heart racing, a knot in your stomach, or a strong urge to act right away.

2. Take a Deep Breath: Before reacting, take a deep breath or even several deep breaths. This helps calm your nervous system and gives you a moment to regain control.

3. Delay Your Response: If possible, take a short break before responding to your partner or the situation. Even a few minutes can give you the space you need to think more clearly and respond thoughtfully.

4. Ask Yourself: What Do I Need Right Now?: In that pause, ask yourself what your real need is. Are you seeking reassurance? Do you need to feel heard? Identifying your need can help you communicate more effectively without reacting impulsively.

In addition to managing those intense moments of emotional flooding, developing long-term emotional independence is key to breaking free from the reliance on external validation. Let's explore how to build a strong sense of self-worth and security that comes from within.

BUILDING EMOTIONAL INDEPENDENCE

For individuals with anxious attachment, there's often a tendency to rely on external sources, such as a partner, friend, or loved one, to regulate emotions. But learning to self-soothe is a valuable tool that can empower you to build emotional independence and reduce your need for constant validation from others.

I used to believe that my emotional well-being was entirely dependent on my partner. Without their constant presence and reassurance, I felt lost and unstable. But through self-regulation, I realized that true security comes from within. I started creating my own emotional safety net by journaling, meditating, and immersing myself in the tranquility of nature with long walks. These practices helped me build a sense of inner peace and resilience that didn't depend on anyone else.

This journey toward emotional independence might look different for everyone, but here are some key strategies that can help you build emotional independence:

1. Create Your Emotional Safety Net: Develop a set of practices or habits that help you feel safe and secure, even when your partner isn't available to provide reassurance. This might include journaling, listening to calming music, practicing deep breathing, or engaging in hobbies that bring you joy and fulfillment.

2. Affirmation Practice: Affirmations can help rewire your internal dialogue and reinforce a sense of self-worth. When anxiety starts to creep in, affirmations like "I am enough," "I can handle this," or "I am worthy of love and respect" can provide comfort and support, helping you manage anxiety without needing external validation.

3. Self-Compassion Exercises: Self-compassion is the practice of treating yourself with kindness and understanding during moments of difficulty. Instead of criticizing yourself for feeling anxious, try showing yourself the same care and support you would give a close friend.

This approach can reduce the shame often associated with anxious attachment behaviors and make it easier for you to manage your emotions.

FINDING STABILITY

Emotional self-regulation isn't just a psychological skill; it's a neurological process. By engaging in practices like grounding exercises, deep breathing, and mindfulness, you activate the parasympathetic nervous system, counteracting the fight-or-flight response triggered by anxiety. This helps to calm your heart rate, relax your muscles, and reduce stress hormones.

At the heart of emotional self-regulation is learning how to maintain internal stability when you feel emotionally flooded. This doesn't mean ignoring or suppressing your emotions. Instead, you're learning to process them in healthy, productive ways. For instance, when you feel overwhelmed by fear that your partner might be pulling away, self-regulation can help you pause, breathe, and gain perspective before reacting impulsively. You begin to replace emotional reactivity with thoughtful responses.

Grounding exercises, engaging in mindfulness, or simply taking a moment to pause are effective tools for managing anxiety in the heat of the moment. These practices help anchor you in the present, allowing your body and mind to settle before engaging with your emotions or partner.

In sum, emotional self-regulation provides a sense of stability necessary for navigating relationships with anxious attachment. It helps you manage your emotions without overwhelming your partner or yourself, creating a healthier, more secure foundation for your connections. As you continue to practice these skills, you'll notice a shift in the way you handle anxiety, leading to more secure and fulfilling relationships.

Developing emotional self-regulation takes time and practice, but with each step forward, you'll find yourself feeling more in control of your emotions and less reliant on others for constant reassurance. This stability not only helps you manage anxious attachment but also allows you to show up in your relationships as a more secure, confident partner.

The next chapter will guide you through techniques to communicate effectively without anxiety, empowering you to express your needs and feelings to strengthen your relationships and avoid triggering insecurity or conflict.

CHAPTER 5: COMMUNICATING WITHOUT ANXIETY

Communication is the foundation of every strong relationship, but for individuals with anxious attachment, it can feel like walking a tightrope. The fear of rejection, abandonment, or unmet expectations amplifies the emotional intensity behind each word spoken, often leading to miscommunications or unspoken needs. Instead of flowing naturally, communication can become a minefield of second-guessing and over-analysis.

Those with anxious attachment may hesitate to speak openly, fearing that being too direct may drive their partner away or that revealing their vulnerabilities could make them seem weak. This fear of being misunderstood or dismissed can result in bottling up emotions, which ultimately leads to frustration and resentment over time.

For example, you might find yourself constantly seeking subtle ways to get reassurance from your partner instead of openly expressing your concerns. Rather than asking directly for what you need, you might engage in indirect communication, hoping they will "just know" how to meet your needs. Unfortunately, this often leads to disappointment when your partner fails to pick up on your cues.

Learning to communicate effectively while managing these anxieties is vital to building healthier, more secure relationships. Communication becomes easier and less fraught with emotional landmines when you can confidently express your needs without being overwhelmed by fear. Instead of approaching conversations from a place of insecurity, you'll begin to cultivate a balanced, assertive approach that fosters mutual understanding and respect.

By the end of this chapter, you'll gain the tools to identify how anxious attachment can sabotage your communication and learn strategies to express yourself in a more grounded, secure manner.

THE PITFALLS OF ANXIOUS COMMUNICATION

When anxiety affects communication, it can prompt behaviors that inadvertently push partners away, even when you're trying to create closeness. It's important to recognize the pitfalls that anxious attachment brings into communication, so you can begin to correct these habits and replace them with positive and constructive strategies.

1. Overcommunication

This happens when anxiety drives you to overexplain your emotions, repeatedly seek reassurance, or ask your partner to constantly validate your feelings.

While it might seem like more communication would bring clarity, it can overwhelm the partner, creating the very distance you're trying to avoid. You may ask your partner questions like, "Do you still love me?" or "Are you upset with me?"—not because anything is necessarily wrong, but because your anxiety creates a need for validation. Over time, this pattern can wear down the relationship, causing your partner to feel burdened by the constant need to reaffirm their feelings.

2. Fear of Confrontation

Anxious individuals might avoid difficult conversations entirely, fearing rejection or abandonment. You might suppress your emotions or let small issues build up, only to erupt later in moments of intense emotion. Avoidance causes misunderstandings and a lack of emotional intimacy in the relationship.

3. Over-Apologizing

Many individuals with anxious attachment tend to over-apologize as a way of preemptively smoothing over conflict, even when they haven't done anything wrong. You might say "I'm sorry" frequently in conversations, especially if you sense tension or fear that your partner is upset. However, over-apologizing diminishes your sense of self-worth and can create an imbalance in the relationship, making your partner feel like they are always being placated rather than addressed honestly.

Understanding these communication pitfalls is the first step in changing how you relate to others. The goal is to move away from reactive, anxiety-driven communication and toward more balanced, thoughtful interactions.

IDENTIFYING YOUR COMMUNICATION STYLE

Before diving into strategies for communicating without anxiety, you should assess where you currently stand. Understanding your communication style is the first step in shifting toward a more balanced, secure way of expressing yourself.

Each person develops a unique way of communicating based on their attachment patterns, past experiences, and relationship dynamics. People with anxious attachment often default to certain communication styles that reflect their deep-seated fears of rejection or abandonment. These styles can hinder healthy interactions, resulting in miscommunication, unresolved conflict, or unmet needs.

Take a moment to reflect on how you typically express yourself in relationships, whether it's with romantic partners, friends, or even family members. Do you often hold back your true feelings to avoid conflict, or do you sometimes react impulsively when anxiety takes over?

Here are four common communication patterns that people with anxious attachment may exhibit. Consider which style resonates with you the most as you read through these descriptions:

- **Passive Communication:**

    If you identify with a passive communication style, you might find yourself avoiding expressing your needs or feelings. You may prioritize maintaining peace over being honest, often out of fear of conflict or rejection. The downside of this approach is experiencing feelings of resentment, frustration, and emotional exhaustion when your needs are unmet. While passivity may seem like a way to avoid confrontation, it often deepens your anxiety, as your emotional needs remain unaddressed.

- **Passive-Aggressive Communication:**

If you tend toward passive-aggressive communication, you may not express your emotions directly but instead use subtle, indirect methods to signal your frustration. This could manifest in behaviors like giving silent treatment, making sarcastic remarks, or leaving underhanded comments. Although you might feel justified, using passive-aggressive communication rarely resolves issues and can escalate conflict due to misunderstandings. Over time, this indirect approach may erode trust and closeness in your relationships.

- **Aggressive Communication:**

  In moments of intense anxiety, you might shift toward aggressive communication. This style is characterized by a need to regain control or protect yourself through forceful or demanding behaviors. Aggressive communication may involve shouting, blaming, or harsh criticisms that push the other person away. While it might feel like a release of pent-up frustration, this approach harms emotional intimacy and can cause the other person to feel attacked or unsafe, deepening the divide in the relationship.

- **Assertive Communication (Goal):**

  Assertive communication is the ideal approach for healthy interactions, which strikes a balance between being passive and aggressive. It allows you to express your needs, thoughts, and emotions clearly, directly, and respectfully. In this style, you take responsibility for your feelings without blaming the other person, and you prioritize mutual understanding.

Assertiveness is rooted in self-confidence and emotional security, allowing both you and your partner to feel heard and valued without fear of judgment or rejection.

Creating positive change requires identifying and understanding your current communication style. Consider how your style may have shaped your past interactions—did you hold back, hoping to keep the peace, only to feel unappreciated or misunderstood later? Or did you express your needs too forcefully, resulting in conflict or pushing people away?

There is no shame in recognizing that your communication may have been shaped by your attachment anxiety. These patterns often develop as coping mechanisms to protect yourself from emotional harm, but they can hold you back from forming secure, fulfilling relationships.

Now that you've reflected on your current style let's explore how to shift toward a more assertive and secure approach—one that empowers you to express your needs without being overwhelmed by fear or the need for constant reassurance.

SPEAKING YOUR NEEDS WITHOUT FEAR

For many people with anxious attachment, asking for what they need feels daunting. You may worry that expressing your desires will burden your partner or push them away. But the truth is, a healthy relationship relies on open communication, and your needs are just as valid as your partner's.

Here are the best ways to start communicating your needs without fear:

1. Use "I" Statements: Instead of framing your needs in a way that might feel accusatory to your partner, use "I" statements to own your feelings. For example, instead of saying, "You never spend time with me," try, "I feel disconnected when we don't spend quality time together." This shifts the focus from blaming your partner to expressing your emotions, creating space for a more productive conversation.

2. Be Direct but Compassionate: It's important to be clear about your needs without being

confrontational. If you need more reassurance, say it calmly and directly: "I've been feeling a bit anxious lately, and it would really help if we could talk about how we're doing."

3. Focus on the Positive: When communicating your needs, frame the conversation around how your partner can support you, rather than focusing on what they're doing wrong. This encourages cooperation rather than defensiveness. For example, instead of saying, "You don't care about my feelings," try, "It would mean a lot to me if we could talk about how I'm feeling right now."

Through these techniques, you'll master expressing your needs in a way that feels safe for you and your partner.

ASSERTIVENESS IN RELATIONSHIPS

Assertiveness is the cornerstone of secure communication. This involves advocating your needs and boundaries while also respecting the needs and boundaries of your partner.

In my own journey, I struggled with assertiveness for years. I would often avoid expressing my needs or opinions for fear of conflict or rejection. This led to resentment and a lack of true intimacy in my relationships. It wasn't until I started practicing assertive communication techniques that I began to experience healthier and more fulfilling connections.

Here's how to practice assertive communication:

1. State Your Needs Clearly

    Assertiveness means being clear and direct about your wants and needs, without being aggressive or demanding. Instead of hinting or hoping your partner will figure it out, be open and honest when expressing yourself.

    Example: Rather than saying, "You never spend time with me," try, "I feel lonely and disconnected when we don't have quality time together. I'd really appreciate it if we could schedule some dedicated time for just the two of us."

2. Use "I" Statements

Again, "I" statements are a powerful communication tool that centers your own thoughts, feelings, and experiences. These statements typically begin with the word "I" and are followed by a description of your emotions or perceptions. For instance, instead of saying, "You always interrupt me," you could say, "I feel frustrated when I'm interrupted."

"I" statements focus on the speaker's thoughts, feelings, and experiences. By using "I" statements, you can express yourself honestly without blaming or accusing the other person. This helps to de-escalate conflict, foster understanding, and create a safe environment for open communication. Remember, taking ownership of your feelings is a crucial step toward establishing healthier and more secure relationships.

3. Set Boundaries Respectfully

Setting boundaries is essential for maintaining your emotional well-being, but it can be challenging when you fear rejection. Remember, a boundary isn't about shutting someone out; it's about defining what is comfortable and acceptable for you.

Example: Instead of saying, "You're always smothering me!", try, "I appreciate your affection, but I need some personal space right now. I'll let you know when I'm ready to reconnect."

4. Be Open to Feedback

Assertiveness is a two-way street. While expressing your own needs and boundaries is necessary, it's equally crucial to listen to your partner's perspective.

Actively listen to their thoughts and feelings and be willing to consider their point of view. This fosters a healthy exchange where both partners feel heard and respected.

Below are three scenarios and effective communication techniques to handle them:

Scenario 1: You feel anxious because your partner hasn't been as communicative lately, making you worry about their commitment to the relationship.

- Ineffective Communication: "You don't care about me anymore. You never text me back, and I feel like you're pulling away."
- Assertive Communication: "I've noticed we haven't been texting as much recently, and I'm feeling a bit anxious about it. Could we talk about how we're both feeling? I miss the connection we usually have, and I want to make sure we're both on the same page."

Scenario 2: Your partner has been spending more time with friends, and you're feeling neglected.

- Ineffective Communication: "You never want to spend time with me anymore. It's like you don't care about us."
- Assertive Communication: "I've noticed that we haven't spent as much time together

recently, and I feel a bit disconnected. I'd really like to plan something where we can reconnect. How about this weekend?"

Scenario 3: You feel overwhelmed by the amount of time your partner wants to spend together and need some personal space.

- Ineffective Communication: "I can't keep hanging out with you all the time. It's too much."
- Assertive Communication: "I love spending time with you, but I've been feeling a little overwhelmed and need some time to recharge. Can we plan some solo time this week so I can be more present when we're together?"

When you're working on being assertive, it's natural to feel vulnerable or anxious about how your partner will respond. Remind yourself that expressing your needs is a healthy and necessary part of building trust and emotional intimacy, even if it feels uncomfortable at first.

If you're looking to dive deeper into practical strategies on how to develop this essential trait, I highly recommend my book *"The Keys to Being Brilliantly Confident and More Assertive: A Vital Guide to Enhancing Your Communication Skills, Getting Rid of Anxiety, and Building Assertiveness."* It offers a comprehensive approach to mastering assertiveness and becoming more self-assured in your interactions.

Navigating Difficult Conversations

Difficult conversations are a normal part of any relationship, whether they involve unfulfilled needs, conflicts, or fears of abandonment. For someone with anxious attachment, these conversations can trigger deep fears of rejection. However, learning to navigate tough conversations with calm and clarity is essential for building secure relationships.

1. Prepare for the Conversation

If you anticipate a difficult conversation, take some time to prepare mentally and emotionally. Reflect on what you want to communicate and why it's important.

Consider how you can express your feelings calmly and clearly without letting anxiety take over.

2. Choose the Right Time and Place

Timing is everything when it comes to discussing sensitive matters. Avoid bringing up certain topics when you and your partner are stressed, in conflict, or exhausted. Instead, choose a time when both of you are calm, relaxed, and able to focus on the discussion.

Make sure to have the conversation in a private, comfortable space where both of you feel safe to express your thoughts without any distractions.

3. Stay Present and Listen

During a difficult conversation, it's easy to get caught up in your emotions or focus solely on what you want to say next. However, effective communication is a two-way street. Make a conscious effort to stay present and listen to your partner's perspective. Avoid interrupting or jumping to conclusions before they've had a chance to fully express their thoughts.

When your partner speaks, practice active listening by nodding, making eye contact, and summarizing what they've said to ensure you understand their point of view. This helps create a more open, empathetic dialogue.

Be aware when you're being emotionally triggered. Pay attention to physical cues—like a racing heart or tension in your body—that signal your anxiety is taking over.

4. Take Breaks If Needed

If the conversation becomes too emotionally charged, taking a break is okay. Emotional flooding can hinder your ability to think clearly and communicate effectively, so it's important to recognize when you need a pause.

Recognizing when you're triggered is crucial to staying grounded. If you feel your heart racing or your mind spinning, take a deep breath and ground yourself by focusing on the present moment. You can also use a simple mindfulness technique, like counting your breaths or paying attention to the sensation of your feet on the floor. These techniques allow your nervous system to calm down, making it easier to respond thoughtfully rather than react impulsively.

After taking a break, rejoin the conversation by calmly restating your goal for the discussion. For example, "I took a moment to calm down, and I'd really like us to continue talking about how we can reconnect." This can keep the conversation on track and prevent escalation.

PRACTICING EMPATHY AND LISTENING

While expressing your needs is vital, communication goes both ways. Unfortunately, those with anxious attachment may struggle to consider the other person's perspective because their own fears and insecurities overpower their ability to empathize. To overcome this challenge and create a more secure communication, learning to practice empathy and active listening is essential.

Here's how to practice empathy in your conversations:

1. Listen Fully Before Responding: When your partner is speaking, focus on understanding their feelings and perspective. Resist the urge to interrupt or start formulating your response while they're talking. Instead, listen carefully to what they're saying and how they're saying it.

2. Reflect Back What You Heard: After your partner has finished speaking, repeat back what you think they said to make sure you understand them correctly. For example, "It sounds like you're feeling frustrated because I've been preoccupied lately. Is that right?" Reflecting back ensures you're on the same page and demonstrates you care about their feelings.

3. Validate Their Emotions: You don't have to agree with everything your partner says, but it's important to acknowledge their emotions. Validation means saying, "I understand why you're feeling this way," without dismissing or minimizing their experience.

4. Practice Compassionate Curiosity: When emotions run high, it's easy to assume the worst. But instead of reacting defensively, try

to stay curious about your partner's experience. Ask open-ended questions like, "Can you tell me more about what you're going through?" Being compassionately curious helps your partner feel safe and understood.

Active listening and empathy are fundamental to building strong, meaningful connections in your relationships. They allow you to truly understand your partner's needs and foster a deeper emotional bond. To master these crucial communication skills and become more attuned to the people in your life, I recommend exploring my book *"The Art of Active Listening: How to Listen Effectively in 10 Simple Steps to Improve Relationships and Increase Productivity."* It provides practical guidance on how to sharpen your listening abilities and create more harmonious, productive relationships.

As you practice assertive communication, embrace vulnerability, and navigate difficult conversations with confidence, you'll create a space for deeper connection, mutual respect, and lasting love.

Remember, the journey toward secure communication is not about suppressing your emotions or pretending you don't have needs. It's about learning to express those needs in a healthy and balanced way that fosters trust and intimacy rather than fear and insecurity.

By incorporating the strategies and techniques outlined in this chapter, you can overcome the patterns of anxious communication that have held you back. You can learn to confidently speak your truth, set boundaries with respect, and handle difficult conversations with grace and resilience. As you do so, you'll not only transform your relationships but also cultivate a deeper sense of self-worth and emotional well-being.

In the next chapter, we'll highlight the complexities of managing intense emotions like jealousy and the fear of abandonment, equipping you with powerful strategies to build greater trust in yourself and your relationships. Remember, healing is a journey, not a destination. With patience, self-compassion, and the tools you're learning, you can create a life where love and connection flourish, free from the grip of anxiety.

153

CHAPTER 6: OVERCOMING JEALOUSY AND FEAR OF ABANDONMENT

Jealousy and fear of abandonment are some of the most challenging emotions for individuals with anxious attachment. They often feel like powerful waves crashing against the foundation of your relationships, leaving you uncertain about whether your bond will hold. The intensity of emotions can make even minor interactions or slight changes in your partner's behavior feel like a threat to your connection.

The important thing to recognize, though, is that while jealousy and abandonment fears feel overwhelming, they don't always reflect the truth. These emotions are often tied to unresolved insecurities or past experiences that color your current relationships. But by learning to manage these emotions, you can build stronger, more trusting connections and, most importantly, find emotional security within yourself.

At its core, jealousy stems from the fear of losing someone you deeply value—the fear that your partner's love, attention, or commitment might slip away. This fear can feel magnified, like your relationships are teetering on the edge. Even innocent situations, such as your partner spending time with friends, engaging in solo hobbies, or working late, can spark intense feelings of insecurity.

These emotional triggers often come from a heightened sensitivity to perceived threats to your relationship. Your mind may quickly jump to worst-case scenarios, imagining your partner drifting away or finding someone else more worthy of their attention. Jealousy then becomes a protective response—an attempt to regain a sense of control over something that feels uncertain.

HOW JEALOUSY MANIFESTS IN ANXIOUS ATTACHMENT

Understanding how jealousy surfaces can help you recognize it in real-time and prevent it from negatively affecting your relationship. Here are a few common ways jealousy manifests:

- Constant Comparisons: You may find yourself constantly comparing your worth to others, such as your partner's friends, coworkers, or even their exes. This comparison game feeds the belief that you're somehow less deserving of their love or attention, intensifying your jealousy.
- Suspicion and Distrust: Even without clear evidence, you might feel suspicious of your partner's motives or actions. You may begin to question whether they're emotionally or physically investing in someone else, which can erode trust.

- Clinginess and Over-Attentiveness: To prevent your partner from pulling away, you might become overly attentive, checking in constantly or seeking constant validation. While closeness is healthy, too much attention can make you and your partner feel emotionally overwhelmed.

- Emotional Outbursts: Jealousy often triggers emotional reactions, such as anger, frustration, or unwarranted accusations. These outbursts come from a place of deep insecurity and fear but can cause harm if they aren't addressed in a healthy way.

Recognizing that jealousy is often a reflection of your own insecurities rather than a response to actual threats is crucial. Jealousy doesn't have to be a destructive force in your relationship. Rather than viewing jealousy as purely negative, see it as an indication of deeper fears or insecurities within yourself that need attention. Jealousy often reflects unresolved wounds—feeling unworthy of love or fearing abandonment. Instead of letting jealousy spiral into conflict, use it as a tool for self-growth.

Ask yourself these questions when jealousy arises:

- **What is my jealousy telling me?**

  Reflect on what triggers your jealousy. Is it your partner's friendship with someone else? Their busy schedule? Ask yourself what these situations stir up in you. Are you afraid your partner will abandon you? Do you fear being replaced by someone "better"? Recognizing the fears beneath your jealousy can help you gain clarity about what you're really afraid of—and it's often not the surface issue you're focused on.

- **Do I believe I'm not enough?**

  One of the core beliefs driving jealousy is the idea that you're not good enough for your partner. This belief assumes that if someone more attractive, successful, or interesting comes along, your partner will lose interest in you. Challenging this belief is crucial for overcoming jealousy. Remind yourself that your partner chose to be with you for a reason, and their affection isn't conditional on superficial traits.

- **Is this based on reality or past experiences?**

Jealousy is often rooted in past experiences, such as inconsistent caregiving, betrayal in previous relationships, or early feelings of abandonment. These past experiences shape your perception of relationships and can cause you to expect rejection, even when it's not warranted. Ask yourself whether your jealousy is based on what's actually happening in your current relationship, or if it's a projection of past hurts. By separating old wounds from present realities, you can start to dismantle the emotional triggers behind your jealousy.

- **How can I transform this into an opportunity for growth?**

  When jealousy arises, reflect on what it's teaching you about your insecurities. Is it telling you that you need to work on building your self-worth? That you need to practice trusting your partner more? Addressing the underlying issues can empower you to shift your mindset from fear to confidence, both in yourself and in your relationship.

Once you acknowledge jealousy as a signal, you can start addressing the insecurities at its core. The goal is not to eliminate jealousy entirely but to understand where it comes from and use that understanding to strengthen your sense of self-worth. By working through the underlying issues, you can build more secure, trusting relationships where jealousy no longer has the power to erode connection.

I once had a close friend who experienced intense jealousy whenever his partner spent time with an attractive coworker. He'd spiral, comparing himself and feeling inadequate. Through our conversations, I helped him realize that this wasn't truly about their partner or the coworker. It was a reflection of his own deep-seated insecurities. After reframing his jealousy as self-doubt, he was able to shift their focus. Instead of trying to control his partner, he began addressing his own need for self-love and acceptance. This shift proved transformative for their relationship and their overall well-being.

My friend's experience highlights the transformative power of reframing jealousy and addressing underlying insecurities. Here are some additional strategies to help you healthily navigate this complex emotion.

MANAGING JEALOUSY IN A HEALTHY WAY

1. Reframe Jealousy as Self-Doubt

Jealousy is often less about your partner's actions and more about your own doubts and insecurities. When you feel jealous, pause and ask yourself: Is this jealousy about them, or is it about me?

For example, if you're feeling jealous because your partner is spending time with someone else, ask yourself if this feeling stems from a lack of trust in your partner or from a fear that you're not "good enough." By reframing jealousy as self-doubt, you can shift your focus away from controlling your partner's behavior and towards addressing your own insecurities.

2. Focus on Building Your Self-Worth

Jealousy thrives in the absence of self-worth. The more secure you feel within yourself, the less likely you're to compare yourself to others or fear that your partner will leave you.

163

Take time to focus on building your self-esteem and self-worth. This could involve practicing affirmations, engaging in activities that bring you joy and confidence, or seeking therapy to work through deeper insecurities. When you feel confident and secure in who you are, the need to compete with others or seek constant reassurance diminishes.

During my personal journey, I discovered that practicing self-compassion and engaging in activities that brought me joy, such as painting and spending time in nature, significantly boosted my self-worth. As my confidence grew, I noticed that feelings of jealousy naturally diminished.

3. Practice Open Communication

Jealousy can often lead to misunderstandings or unspoken resentment. Instead of letting jealousy fester, communicate your feelings with your partner in a calm and constructive way.

For example, instead of accusing your partner of not caring or spending too much time with someone else, express how you're feeling in a non-blaming way: "I've

164

been feeling a little insecure lately, and I think it's making me more sensitive to how much time we're spending together. Can we talk about how we can reconnect more?"

In a past relationship, I struggled with communicating my feelings of jealousy. I'd often bottle them up, afraid of seeming "needy" or "clingy." This only led to resentment and misunderstandings. Eventually, I learned to express my concerns calmly and honestly, focusing on how their actions made me feel rather than accusing them of wrongdoing. This opened up a dialogue that allowed us to address the root of my jealousy and build a stronger foundation of trust.

When you communicate your feelings without making accusations, you invite your partner to understand your perspective and offer reassurance in a healthy way.

4. Build Trust

Trust is the antidote to jealousy. Building trust in your relationship requires consistent communication, honesty, and openness. One way to strengthen trust is by practicing trust-building exercises with your partner. This could involve:

- Sharing Vulnerabilities: Take time to share your fears, insecurities, and needs with your partner in a safe and supportive environment.

- Setting Boundaries: Establish clear boundaries around communication, time spent with others, and relationship expectations, so both you and your partner feel secure.

- Checking In Regularly: Make it a habit to check in with each other regularly, which could mean weekly, bi-weekly, or monthly, depending on the needs of your relationship. These check-ins should be intentional conversations where you both discuss how you're feeling about the relationship, address any concerns, and express appreciation. This allows you to address issues early and maintain a healthy connection before jealousy or conflicts escalate.

Addressing the Fear of Abandonment

At the heart of anxious attachment is often a deep-seated fear of abandonment. You may constantly worry that your partner will leave you, cheat on you, or simply stop caring. This fear can lead to clingy behavior, overthinking, and emotional outbursts—all of which can ironically push your partner away.

As mentioned before, it's important to recognize that the fear of abandonment is often more about your own insecurities than it is about your partner's behavior. Learning to address this fear internally can help you break free from the cycle of anxiety and build a stronger sense of trust in your relationship.

Let's explore three powerful strategies to help you dismantle the fear of abandonment and build a stronger sense of security within yourself and your relationships.

1. Challenge Your Assumptions

One effective way to deal with the fear of abandonment is to challenge the assumptions that fuel it. When you start thinking thoughts like, "They're going to leave me," or "I'm not important to them," ask yourself: Is this assumption based on fact, or is it driven by my fear?

For example, if your partner doesn't text you back right away, instead of assuming they've lost interest, challenge that assumption by considering other possibilities: "They're probably just busy right now," or "We've had great communication so far, and this doesn't mean they don't care."

Questioning your assumptions can stop anxiety from taking over, allowing you to gain a more balanced perspective on the situation.

2. Develop Emotional Independence

The fear of abandonment often stems from a belief that your emotional well-being is tied to your partner's presence or validation. While relationships are an integral source of emotional support, it's crucial to cultivate emotional independence—the ability to self-soothe and regulate your emotions without relying solely on your partner.

For years, I relied on my partner for security and validation. Any time I was single, I felt lost and anxious. However, I learned that true security comes from within. By exploring new hobbies, deepening friendships, and prioritizing self-care, I developed a sense of wholeness that didn't depend on external validation or a romantic relationship.

Building emotional independence can involve:

- Practicing Self-Soothing: Learn techniques like deep breathing, mindfulness, or journaling to calm yourself when anxiety strikes.
- Engaging in Self-Care: Prioritize activities that nurture your emotional well-being, such as exercise, hobbies, or spending time with friends and family.
- Setting Boundaries with Yourself: When you feel the urge to reach out for reassurance, practice pausing and asking yourself, "Can I

find reassurance within myself in this moment?"

3. Trust Your Relationship

One of the biggest challenges in overcoming the fear of abandonment is learning to trust in the strength of your relationship. It's natural to feel vulnerable when you care deeply about someone, but constantly worrying about losing them can create unnecessary strain on the relationship and on yourself.

Remind yourself of the positive aspects of your relationship and the ways in which your partner has shown their commitment. Trust is built over time, and by focusing on the stability and consistency of your relationship, you can let go of the fear that your relationship is constantly on the verge of falling apart.

For those with anxious attachment, jealousy and the fear of abandonment can feel like constant shadows, lurking in the background of your relationships. While these emotions are powerful, they don't have to control your narrative. By working on building trust—both in yourself and your partner—you can foster a sense of emotional security.

Begin by recognizing jealousy as a sign that there's inner work to do, rather than letting it spiral into destructive behavior. As you focus on cultivating self-worth, communicating openly, and challenging your fears, you'll notice a gradual shift. The anxiety that once dominated your thoughts will begin to recede, replaced by a growing sense of security.

In the next chapter, we'll explore how to break free from reassurance-seeking behavior, another common pattern in anxious attachment. You'll learn how to cultivate emotional self-reliance, which is vital to developing truly secure attachments.

CHAPTER 7: BREAKING FREE FROM REASSURANCE-SEEKING BEHAVIOR

Imagine sitting with your partner at a social gathering, but instead of enjoying the moment, you're hyper-focused on their interactions with others. Every laugh they share with someone else, every glance away from you feels like an unsettling shift in the relationship. The thoughts creep in: *Are they more interested in them than me? Am I enough?*

For those with anxious attachment, seeking reassurance is like living with a constant background hum of unease—where even neutral situations can trigger a flood of insecurity. You might find yourself overanalyzing your partner's behaviors, desperately searching for signs of approval or affection to quiet the storm of doubt inside. But this relentless need for reassurance can often push your partner away, creating a cycle that leaves both of you feeling emotionally drained.

Research shows that individuals with anxious attachment often misread these neutral or positive social cues as threatening, escalating their need for validation. In this chapter, we'll uncover ways to shift the focus from seeking external reassurance to cultivating internal security, so you can break free from this cycle and foster healthier, more balanced relationships.

WHY DO WE SEEK REASSURANCE?

Reassurance-seeking stems from insecurity and fear, particularly the fear of unpredictability in relationships. If you have an anxious attachment style, you may feel uncertain about your partner's love or worry that their feelings might change suddenly. This uncertainty drives the urge to check in frequently, seeking confirmation that you're still loved, valued, and significant.

When you ask for reassurance and receive it—whether through words, actions, or affection—it can temporarily soothe your anxiety. For a brief moment, the fear of abandonment fades, and you feel secure again. But this relief doesn't last. Within hours or days, doubts resurface: "Do they really love me? Are they going to leave? Do I still matter to them?" This leads to more reassurance-seeking behavior, reinforcing the anxiety-reassurance cycle.

This cycle becomes addictive, as each instance of reassurance provides short-term relief but leaves the deeper fears unaddressed. As a result, the anxiety always returns, making reassurance-seeking a habitual response to emotional insecurity.

WHY REASSURANCE DOESN'T OFFER LASTING SECURITY

While reassurance-seeking may seem like a way to calm your fears, it ultimately doesn't provide long-term emotional security. Instead, it often reinforces anxiety and undermines emotional independence. Here's why:

1. Reassurance Is External

Reassurance relies on someone else to provide you with a sense of security. While seeking comfort from loved ones is natural, relying heavily on external validation can create an unhealthy dynamic where your emotional well-being depends on how others respond, hindering your internal emotional resilience.

2. Reassurance Is Short-Lived

Even when your partner reassures you, the relief is often fleeting. The underlying doubts and fears fueling your anxious attachment remain unaddressed, leading to a cycle of temporary calm followed by recurring anxiety. Without addressing the deeper emotional insecurities, reassurance becomes a quick fix rather than a long-term solution.

3. Reassurance Can Strain Relationships

Your partner may feel overwhelmed by the constant demands for validation or frustrated by the fact that no amount of reassurance seems to be enough. Over time, this can lead to tension, misunderstandings, and emotional distance in the relationship.

For example, think about the relationship between Ross and Rachel on Friends. Throughout their on-again, off-again romance, Ross's insecurities often led him to seek constant reassurance from Rachel. Whether it was about her feelings for other men or their time apart, his need for validation caused numerous conflicts, most notably the infamous "we were on a break" incident. The constant reassurance-seeking didn't just strain their relationship; it fueled misunderstandings and created emotional distance, leaving both partners frustrated and hurt.

Now that we understand how reassurance-seeking undermines emotional security, let's explore how you can start breaking free from this behavior.

TRUSTING YOUR RELATIONSHIP WITHOUT CONSTANT REASSURANCE

A crucial step in breaking free from reassurance-seeking is learning to trust in your relationship and yourself. Trust isn't built overnight, but with consistent actions from you and your partner, it becomes the foundation of emotional security.

1. Build Trust in Your Partner

Trust grows through consistent behavior. If you're in a healthy relationship, focus on the ways your partner has shown love and care in the past. This helps reinforce the belief that your connection is strong, even in moments of doubt. Start a "Trust Journal," where you jot down moments when your partner demonstrated their commitment, such as helping you during a difficult time or supporting your goals. This simple practice can become a powerful reminder when insecurity creeps in.

2. Strengthen Emotional Boundaries

Having healthy emotional boundaries is vital to breaking the cycle of reassurance-seeking. Emotional boundaries help you maintain a sense of self and emotional stability, even when your partner is unavailable or distant.

- Give Yourself Space: When you feel the urge to seek reassurance, practice giving yourself space. Instead of immediately reaching out to your partner, take a moment to breathe, reflect, and self-soothe. This space allows you to regain emotional balance without relying on your partner's response.
- Respect Your Partner's Boundaries: If your partner is busy or unavailable, practice patience and remind yourself that their temporary absence doesn't mean they've stopped caring.

3. Develop Emotional Resilience

Emotional resilience means being able to handle emotional challenges without immediately seeking external validation. Start with small exercises, like practicing mindfulness to stay present when feelings of insecurity arise. Journaling about your thoughts and fears is another way to process emotions without reacting impulsively. Each time you manage these feelings on your own, you strengthen your ability to cope with anxiety independently.

CULTIVATING EMOTIONAL INDEPENDENCE

Taking the initiative to break free from the habit of constant reassurance-seeking is a powerful step toward emotional independence. By learning to validate your own feelings, build self-confidence, and trust in your relationship, you can effectively diminish your reliance on external validation and develop a more secure, self-reliant mindset.

The process of letting go of reassurance-seeking takes time and practice, but each step you take toward self-validation is a step toward greater emotional freedom. You'll find that as you trust yourself more, the need for constant validation fades, and you become more confident in your relationships and your ability to navigate emotional challenges.

In the next chapter, we'll focus on building secure relationships, offering tools and strategies to foster emotional security and mutual trust with your partner while continuing to heal from anxious attachment.

A Short Message from the Author

Hi, are you enjoying the book thus far? I'd love to hear your thoughts! Many readers do not know how hard reviews are to come by and how much they help an author.

I would be incredibly thankful if you could take just 30 seconds to write a brief review on Amazon, even if it's just a few sentences!

Thank you for taking the time to share your thoughts!

CHAPTER 8: BUILDING SECURE RELATIONSHIPS

Reaching the point where you can build secure, healthy relationships is a major milestone in recovering from anxious attachment. This journey takes courage, patience, and vulnerability, and arriving at this stage is worth celebrating.

Anxious attachment often creates cycles of insecurity, where the need for reassurance destabilizes the relationship. But with intention, practice, and the right tools, you can replace these patterns with behaviors that promote stability and build trust. Building a secure relationship is a gradual process, but as you learn to trust yourself and your partner, it becomes more natural. In this chapter, we'll discuss how to create secure bonds, repair relationships affected by anxious attachment, and foster long-term trust.

CHOOSING THE RIGHT PARTNER

Choosing the right partner can feel like you're torn between what you believe you deserve and what you're afraid of losing. The emotional toll can be draining—each unreturned message and every moment of distance amplifies your fears of rejection, leaving you wondering if you're truly worthy of the meaningful connection you crave.

Letting go of emotionally unavailable partners requires not only recognizing that they don't meet your needs but also confronting the underlying fear that their distance is somehow your fault. It's common to think, "If I were more loveable, they wouldn't pull away," or "Maybe if I just try harder, they'll open up." These thoughts can make it incredibly difficult to detach from unhealthy relationships, as the desire to gain their approval

184

and emotional availability becomes a reflection of your own self-worth.

This emotional struggle can feel like a battle between your head and your heart. On one hand, you know that being involved with someone who is inconsistent or avoidant isn't healthy for you. On the other hand, the idea of walking away can feel like you're admitting defeat—like you've failed to secure their affection. For someone with anxious attachment, this can be deeply triggering, reigniting feelings of unworthiness and abandonment.

Recognizing that an emotionally unavailable partner's distance is not a reflection of your value is important. As we've discussed in previous chapters, emotional unavailability often stems from the partner's own attachment style or past experiences, not from anything you've done wrong. Understanding this allows you to detach without internalizing their behavior as a personal failure.

185

If your partner frequently withdraws during emotionally intense moments, it may not be because you're asking too much. They could have learned to cope with intimacy by keeping people at a distance. This realization can help ease the emotional burden you place on yourself to "fix" the relationship.

One way to manage these emotions is to refocus on what *you* need in a relationship. When you prioritize finding a partner who is emotionally available, consistent, and supportive, you shift the focus from trying to win over someone who isn't capable of meeting your needs to finding someone who can. While this shift can feel daunting—especially if you've spent a long time in relationships that mirror unhealthy dynamics—it's essential for your emotional well-being.

What to Look for in a Secure Partner

To avoid falling into unhealthy patterns, focus on finding a partner who:

186

- **Communicates consistently**: They show up when they say they will, follow through on promises, and communicate openly without leaving you guessing.
- **Is emotionally available**: They are comfortable engaging in meaningful conversations about feelings, needs, and the future of the relationship.
- **Respects your boundaries**: They honor your emotional and physical boundaries without pushing you into uncomfortable situations.

Letting go of emotionally unavailable partners may feel like a loss, but it's a necessary step in creating space for a partner who is capable of meeting you where you are emotionally. The process can trigger feelings of rejection, abandonment, and self-doubt, but keep in mind that their emotional unavailability is not about you—it's about them.

By choosing an emotionally available partner, you

187

create a foundation for a secure relationship where your needs are met, your boundaries are respected, and the constant cycle of reassurance-seeking is no longer necessary. This shift allows you to move from a place of anxiety to a place of security, where you can foster trust, mutual respect, and emotional intimacy.

RED FLAGS

While finding a partner who meets your emotional needs is essential, it's equally important to recognize warning signs that may indicate emotional unavailability or avoidant behaviors. These red flags can often exacerbate anxious attachment, leaving you feeling insecure, confused, or even questioning your worth. Understanding why people exhibit these behaviors—and how to spot them—helps you avoid unhealthy relationship patterns before they take root.

Emotional unavailability or avoidant behavior can stem from various causes, often rooted in a person's past experiences or attachment style. Someone with avoidant attachment may have grown up in an

188

environment where vulnerability was discouraged or even punished, leading them to associate emotional closeness with discomfort or fear. They might protect themselves by keeping emotional distance from others, consciously or unconsciously pushing people away when intimacy overwhelms them.

On the surface, these behaviors might seem like inconsistency or lack of interest, but they are often mechanisms to avoid potential emotional pain or rejection. Understanding the underlying reasons behind these behaviors is crucial. For someone with anxious attachment, this kind of partner can be particularly triggering, as their emotional distance mirrors your deepest fears—abandonment, rejection, or unreciprocated affection.

- Inconsistent Communication:

  It can be incredibly tough for people with anxious attachment when the person they're close to is sometimes super attentive and then completely distant at other times. This kind of push-and-pull behavior can be really destabilizing. In many cases, they may genuinely want connection but become overwhelmed by emotional intimacy, leading them to retreat. Pay attention to patterns over time. If your partner frequently disappears after moments of closeness or avoids deeper conversations following emotional exchanges, this may indicate an avoidant attachment pattern.

How to Handle It:

Instead of rushing to seek reassurance in these moments of distance, observe the pattern. Ask yourself whether this inconsistency is driven by something circumstantial (such as stress or work) or if it's a repeated behavior. Initiate a conversation with your partner, but don't assume the responsibility of trying to "fix" their communication. Their avoidance isn't your fault, and you can't resolve it on your own.

- Avoidance of Emotional Intimacy:

  Some individuals avoid emotional intimacy, steering clear of deep conversations about feelings, relationships, or future plans. This avoidance may be a sign of emotional unavailability, which is often driven by a fear of vulnerability or rejection. People who struggle with intimacy may feel more comfortable keeping relationships superficial and maintaining a "safe" distance to avoid emotional entanglement.

How to Handle It:

If you notice your partner regularly evades meaningful conversations about emotions or the future, take this as a significant red flag, especially for someone with an anxious attachment style. You might constantly try to push for a deeper connection, only to feel rejected when your partner pulls away. In this situation, try having an honest conversation where you express your need for emotional intimacy. If your partner continues to avoid these discussions or dismiss your feelings, they may not be ready or willing to build the level of connection you need.

- Frequent Canceling or Flaking on Plans:

Regularly canceled plans or a general lack of follow-through on commitments is a clear sign that someone may not be fully invested in the relationship. This behavior often suggests that they are either uncertain about their feelings or unwilling to prioritize the connection. For someone with avoidant tendencies, canceling plans may serve as a way to maintain emotional distance and keep their autonomy intact, avoiding the closeness that regular interaction would create.

How to Handle It:

Chronic canceling can lead to feelings of insecurity, causing you to question your partner's commitment or feelings toward you. Instead of internalizing the blame, consider that this behavior might have more to do with their fear of commitment than anything you're doing wrong. If their cancellations continue without valid reasons or effort to reschedule, it might be time to reconsider whether this relationship can offer the consistency you need to feel secure.

- Reluctance to Define the Relationship:

Hesitancy to label the relationship or express commitment is often a significant red flag, particularly if your partner avoids conversations about exclusivity or long-term plans. Avoidant partners may resist defining the relationship because they fear losing their independence or becoming "trapped" in emotional obligations. This reluctance leaves you, as someone with anxious attachment, feeling unsettled and uncertain about the future of the relationship.

How to Handle It:

If your partner frequently sidesteps discussions about where the relationship is heading, evaluate whether their reluctance aligns with your emotional needs. You deserve clarity and commitment if that's what you seek. Have a candid conversation about your expectations, but be prepared to make difficult choices if your partner is unable to provide the emotional security you need.

For individuals with anxious attachment, emotional unavailability can exacerbate anxiety and make it harder to feel secure in relationships. Recognizing these red flags early helps protect you from investing deeply in relationships that don't offer the emotional connection you deserve. More importantly, understanding the reasons behind these behaviors empowers you to make informed decisions.

Rather than chasing after someone who triggers your fears, you can step back and ask, "Is this person capable of offering the emotional intimacy I need?" Being aware of these patterns also helps you avoid falling into a cycle of self-blame, realizing that your partner's emotional unavailability is about their own attachment style or emotional limitations—not your inadequacy.

When you prioritize emotional availability in a partner, you create the space for a secure, supportive relationship where trust can thrive. You're less likely to feel the constant need for reassurance, and instead, you can build a relationship based on mutual respect, understanding, and emotional intimacy.

CREATING SECURE BONDS IN NEW RELATIONSHIPS

Entering a new relationship can bring excitement and hope, but for someone recovering from anxious attachment, it can also stir up old fears. The uncertainty might trigger your doubts, leading you to seek reassurance or over-analyze your partner's actions. But by applying the tools you've learned in your recovery, you can approach new relationships with a secure mindset.

A secure relationship is built on intention and awareness. Instead of falling into patterns of seeking validation or overthinking, focus on creating a foundation based on mutual respect and trust.

SETTING HEALTHY BOUNDARIES

Boundaries are essential for creating secure relationships and serve as protective measures that safeguard your emotional well-being. They ensure that both you and your partner feel respected and valued. However, for individuals with anxious attachment, setting boundaries can feel especially challenging. The idea of asserting your needs may trigger fears of rejection, abandonment, or conflict, so you tend to avoid boundary-setting, as it may bring up feelings of insecurity or unworthiness.

Why Boundaries Feel Risky for Anxious Individuals

At the heart of anxious attachment is the deep fear that setting a boundary will push your partner away. You might worry that asserting your needs could make you seem "difficult" or "too much," causing your partner to pull back or even leave. These fears often stem from past experiences where your emotional needs were dismissed, neglected, or met with rejection. As a result, you may feel compelled to prioritize your partner's needs over your own in an effort to secure their affection.

But here's the paradox: neglecting your own needs in an attempt to keep your partner close often leads to emotional burnout, resentment, and further insecurity. Healthy boundaries are not about pushing someone away but are about creating space for mutual respect and emotional intimacy to thrive. When you set boundaries, you show yourself and your partner that your needs matter, paving the way for a balanced, secure relationship.

Emotional Challenges in Boundary-Setting

1. Fear of Rejection:

   One of the most common emotional hurdles anxious individuals face when setting boundaries is the fear that their partner will view their needs as burdensome. This fear can cause you to minimize your needs or avoid boundary-setting entirely. However, it's important to recognize that this fear is often rooted in past experiences, not necessarily reflective of your current relationship. Your partner will not automatically leave because you assert yourself—especially if they value and respect you.

How to Manage It:

Before having a boundary-setting conversation, take time to remind yourself that healthy boundaries are necessary for relationship health. Affirm that you are worthy of having your needs met and that a secure relationship will accommodate those needs. A simple mantra like, "My needs are valid, and a healthy relationship will respect them," can help ground you emotionally before entering the conversation.

2. People-Pleasing Tendencies:

People-pleasing is a common coping mechanism for those with anxious attachment. Prioritizing your partner's comfort over your own needs might create temporary peace but ultimately leads to resentment and emotional exhaustion.

How to Manage It:

Recognize that true emotional intimacy cannot exist without mutual respect for boundaries. Practice reframing boundary-setting as an act of self-respect rather than a confrontation. If you find yourself hesitating to set a boundary because you fear displeasing your partner, pause and ask yourself: "What will happen if I continue to neglect my own needs?" This shift in perspective can help you prioritize your emotional well-being.

3. Feeling Selfish or Guilty:

For many anxious individuals, setting boundaries can bring up feelings of guilt or selfishness. You may think, I'm asking for too much," or "I don't want to burden them." However, healthy boundaries are not acts of selfishness; they are acts of self-care. Distinguishing between being assertive and being demanding is essential. Boundaries are about taking responsibility for your emotional health and ensuring your needs are respected.

How to Manage It:

Acknowledge the guilt when it arises, but challenge it. Remind yourself that boundaries are necessary for maintaining emotional health—not just yours, but your partner's as well. In fact, setting boundaries often makes relationships stronger because both partners feel they can be authentic without sacrificing their well-being. Practice self-compassion by reminding yourself that caring for your emotional needs isn't selfish—it's necessary for a healthy relationship.

How to Set Boundaries with Emotional Awareness

1. Be Clear and Direct, Yet Compassionate:

When setting a boundary, be clear and direct, but also compassionate toward yourself and your partner. Avoid vague statements that leave room for misinterpretation, which can lead to confusion or frustration. At the same time, understand that asserting a boundary may feel uncomfortable, and that's okay. Healthy boundaries foster respect, not distance.

Example: Instead of saying, "I feel like I need more space sometimes," you might say, "I'm usually swamped with work during the week and need my weekends to recharge, so I might not always be up for hanging out." This version is direct, specific, and expresses your needs without leaving room for misunderstanding. You can also express empathy by acknowledging the impact of the boundary: "I understand this might change how often we see each other, but I believe it will help me feel more balanced and present in our relationship."

2. Respect Your Partner's Boundaries:

Healthy relationships are reciprocal, meaning that you must respect your partner's just as you expect them to respect yours. Respecting boundaries is key to fostering trust, as it shows that both individuals are valued equally. If your partner expresses a need for space, downtime, or emotional processing, try not to interpret it as rejection but as a necessary part of maintaining their well-being.

How to Manage It:

If your partner sets a boundary that triggers your anxiety, take a moment to reflect before you react. Remind yourself that boundaries are not personal—they are about your partner's needs. Practice emotional regulation techniques, such as deep breathing or journaling, to process any feelings of insecurity that arise. This allows you to respond with understanding rather than panic.

3. Revisit Boundaries as the Relationship Evolves:

Boundaries aren't static; they need to evolve with the relationship. As you and your partner grow closer, your emotional needs may change. Make the effort to regularly check in with each other to ensure both of your needs are still being met. Relationships thrive when there's an ongoing dialogue about what's working and what needs to be adjusted.

How to Manage It:

Initiate periodic conversations about boundaries, framing them as check-ins rather than confrontations. For example, you might say, "I wanted to revisit how we've been balancing time together and time apart. I'm wondering if we're both feeling comfortable with our current dynamic." This approach creates a space for open communication without making the conversation feel tense or accusatory.

BUILDING TRUST AND SECURITY

Trust is the bedrock of any secure relationship. Without it, relationships may feel unsteady, fueling anxiety, doubt, and emotional insecurity. Building emotional trust requires consistency, honesty, and vulnerability—qualities that forge a strong bond and provide the reassurance both partners need to feel safe.

For individuals with anxious attachment, the fear of being abandoned or hurt can make it tough to fully trust a partner, especially in the early stages of a relationship. However, trust doesn't have to be built all at once. By consistently taking small steps and maintaining open communication, you can gradually build trust, laying a foundation of emotional safety and stability.

WAYS TO BUILD EMOTIONAL TRUST:

- Communicate Openly:

  Open and honest communication is essential for building trust. In a new relationship, being transparent about your feelings, needs, and expectations is vital. If you're feeling anxious or unsure, express it calmly and without blame.

  For example, you might say, "I've been feeling a bit anxious about how we communicate, and I'd love it if we could check in with each other more often." By expressing your concerns in a non-confrontational way, you open the door for constructive dialogue, allowing both partners to address any issues together.

- Show Consistency in Your Actions:

  Trust is built through consistent actions over time. This means following through on your commitments, showing up when you say you will, and being dependable in your words and actions. Establishing a pattern of reliability is especially important in a new relationship.

Consistency builds a sense of safety, proving that you and your partner can rely on each other, even in moments of uncertainty or conflict.

- Encourage Vulnerability:

  Vulnerability is at the heart of emotional intimacy. By being open and vulnerable with your partner, you create a safe space for them to share their own feelings and fears as well. This deepens the emotional bond and fosters a sense of closeness and trust.

  If you're used to guarding your emotions, vulnerability may feel uncomfortable, but it's a crucial step in building a secure connection.

By setting healthy boundaries, building emotional trust, and fostering open communication, you lay the groundwork for a relationship that is not only secure but also deeply fulfilling. As you navigate these early stages with confidence and clarity, you can shift from anxious attachment patterns to secure, balanced behaviors that promote long-lasting connection and emotional security.

LEARNING TO TRUST AGAIN

The fear of abandonment, betrayal, or emotional neglect may overshadow even the healthiest relationships, leading to constant doubt and mistrust. Rebuilding trust—whether in your partner or in yourself—takes time and effort, especially when trust has been repeatedly compromised. However, learning to trust again is crucial for creating lasting, secure connections and freeing yourself from the anxiety that once dominated your relationships.

First, it's essential to acknowledge that trust is a process, not a one-time event. For individuals working through anxious attachment, rebuilding trust may feel overwhelming, especially when old patterns of doubt resurface. You may experience setbacks or moments of uncertainty, but that doesn't mean trust is unattainable. Trust is built through consistent actions, open communication, and a commitment to growth. Like any relationship skill, trust grows over time.

When trust is broken, whether by betrayal, dishonesty, or emotional neglect, it can shake the very foundation of a relationship. However, with a shared commitment to repair, it's possible to rebuild trust and create a stronger, more secure connection. The following steps are designed to help you and your partner navigate the difficult process of trust repair.

1. Open Dialogue: Acknowledge the Breach of Trust

    The first step in rebuilding trust is to openly acknowledge that it has been broken. This is not a time for avoidance or deflection. Both partners should have a transparent conversation about what happened and how it affected the relationship.

    For the person who broke the trust, taking responsibility is crucial. While a sincere apology is beneficial, it must go beyond words. The partner who caused the breach needs to express an understanding of how their actions hurt their partner and communicate a willingness to make amends.

For Example:

"I realize that lying about where I was last night caused you to feel betrayed, and I understand why that has shaken your trust in me. I am committed to rebuilding that trust through honesty and openness moving forward."

For the partner whose trust was broken, expressing your hurt and concerns is equally important. Avoiding the issue may temporarily prevent conflict, but it will leave unresolved emotions festering beneath the surface. Use "I" statements to express your feelings without blaming your partner.

For Example:

"I feel deeply hurt and unsure about our relationship after discovering that you were not truthful with me. I want us to work through this, but it's going to take time for me to trust again."

2. Set Clear and New Boundaries

When trust has been broken, it often signals the need to revisit the boundaries of the relationship. Setting clear, new boundaries can help create a sense of security moving forward, allowing both partners to understand the expectations moving forward. Establishing these boundaries can also prevent the issue from recurring and give both partners a framework for rebuilding the relationship on stronger, more transparent ground.

For Example:

- After a breach involving dishonesty: You and your partner might agree on more open communication regarding social plans or financial decisions.
- After a breach involving infidelity: Boundaries around communication

with third parties or specific actions that led to the breach may need to be redefined to restore confidence.

How to Manage It:

When setting new boundaries, focus on creating a structure that fosters security rather than restricting freedom. Discuss these boundaries openly and check in regularly to ensure they continue to meet both of your needs as the relationship progresses. Boundaries aren't about controlling one another—they're about ensuring both partners feel emotionally safe moving forward.

Example:

"Given what happened, I think it would help me rebuild trust if we agreed to be more transparent about our plans and who we're spending time with. It's not about control, but about helping me feel more secure as we move forward."

3. Rebuild Trust Through Consistent Actions

Words alone cannot rebuild trust—consistent, reliable actions are vital. The partner who broke the trust must demonstrate, through their behavior, that they are committed to earning back their partner's faith. This entails following through on promises, being emotionally available, and showing a commitment to repairing the relationship.

For the partner whose trust was broken, rebuilding trust requires patience and an openness to seeing your partner's efforts. It's natural to feel skeptical at first but allow yourself to notice and acknowledge the positive changes your partner is making. Over time, these consistent actions will start to reinforce the sense of trust that was lost.

Example:
If your partner has been unreliable with communication in the past, consistent actions could mean regularly checking in when they say they will and being open about their

whereabouts. Over time, this consistency rebuilds a sense of safety and reliability in the relationship.

4. Practice Forgiveness (But Don't Rush It)

While forgiveness is an essential part of trust repair, keep in mind that forgiveness is a process—it doesn't happen overnight. It's perfectly normal to take time to forgive your partner fully, especially if the breach of trust was significant. Rushing forgiveness before you're emotionally ready can lead to resentment down the line.

How to Approach It:

Give yourself permission to feel hurt, angry, or upset. Don't suppress those emotions in an attempt to speed up the healing process. At the same time, communicate with your partner about your journey toward forgiveness and what you need to feel supported as you work through it. Genuine forgiveness requires emotional processing, and when both partners understand this, the prospect of healing becomes smoother.

Example:
"I'm working on forgiving you, but it's going to take time. I need us to continue having open conversations and space to process my emotions. I appreciate your patience as we work through this."

5. Reaffirm Commitment to Growth

Finally, for trust to be rebuilt, both partners must commit to ongoing growth. This involves continually checking in with each other, keeping communication open, and nurturing the relationship over time. Trust isn't something you rebuild once and forget—it requires continuous effort to maintain. Periodic discussions about what's working, what needs adjusting, and how both partners feel can help ensure that trust remains strong.

How to Maintain It:

Schedule regular check-ins with your partner about your relationship's emotional health. Make space for honest conversations about how you're both feeling and whether any adjustments are needed to sustain the trust you've rebuilt.

Example:

"We've been doing better, and I feel more secure than before. But I think it's important that we keep checking in to make sure we're both feeling good about how things are progressing. Maybe we can have monthly conversations about how we feel in the relationship."

BUILDING LONG-TERM TRUST: A COMMITMENT TO HEALING

Learning to trust again after it's been broken is one of the most challenging aspects of recovering from anxious attachment. However, through open dialogue, new boundaries, consistent actions, and a commitment to growth, trust can be restored and strengthened. It's crucial to remember that trust is not a one-time achievement; it's something both partners need to nurture consistently through their actions and communication.

By taking these steps, you'll create a foundation for a healthier, more secure connection—one built on mutual respect, emotional safety, and trust that both you and your partner are committed to maintaining over time.

REPAIRING RELATIONSHIPS DAMAGED BY ANXIOUS ATTACHMENT

Repairing a relationship strained or damaged by anxious attachment is a necessary and courageous step for many. Often, individuals with anxious attachment may not realize how their behaviors, driven by deep-seated fears of abandonment and rejection, impact their partners. Over time, repeated cycles of reassurance-seeking, emotional outbursts, or withdrawal may erode trust, communication, and emotional connection. However, repairing these relationships is possible, and the work invested can lead to an even stronger and more secure bond.

Why Is Repairing the Relationship Important?

Acknowledging and repairing the damage caused by anxious attachment is essential for a few reasons:

- **Restoring Emotional Trust:** Relationships thrive on trust, and trust is often one of the first casualties when attachment anxiety is present. Repairing this trust helps both partners feel safe and valued in the relationship.
- **Fostering Emotional Growth:** Addressing the underlying causes of anxious behaviors allows both partners to grow emotionally. For the individual with anxious attachment, it can be a chance to gain insight into their insecurities and find healthier ways to express their needs. For their partner, it offers a deeper understanding of the anxious individual's experience and a chance to work toward greater empathy and patience.
- **Breaking Negative Cycles:** Without repair, anxious attachment patterns can lead to a cycle of negativity that perpetuates feelings of insecurity

217

and dissatisfaction for both partners. This can cause further emotional damage and, in many cases, may even lead to the dissolution of the relationship. By repairing the damage, the couple can break free from this destructive cycle and build a new foundation of mutual respect and understanding.

- **Strengthening the Bond:** Repairing the relationship not only heals past wounds but also strengthens the emotional bond between partners. By addressing difficult issues head-on and working through them together, couples can create deeper emotional intimacy and resilience, which will serve them well in future challenges.

STEPS TO REPAIR A DAMAGED RELATIONSHIP

To repair a relationship affected by anxious attachment, both partners need to be committed to the process. Here's how you can work together to rebuild and fortify the connection:

1. Acknowledge the Impact

The first step in repairing any relationship is acknowledging the impact anxious attachment has had on the dynamic. This requires honesty and vulnerability from both partners. The person with anxious attachment should acknowledge how their behaviors have contributed to the tension, while their partner can reflect on their own reactions. You aren't placing blame but taking responsibility and creating a space for open communication.

For example, you might say, "I realize that my need for constant reassurance has been overwhelming for you, and I want to work on finding more balance in how I express my needs."

For their partner, recognizing how they may have reacted to those behaviors—perhaps with frustration or withdrawal—can also open the door to healing.

2. Create a Space for Honest Communication

Open communication is key to mending a damaged relationship. Create a safe space where both partners can express their thoughts, feelings, and fears without judgment. Practice active listening and focus on understanding each other rather than assigning blame.

For example, the partner with anxious attachment might say: "I realize that my need for constant reassurance has been overwhelming. I'm worried about losing you, but I'm working on trusting us more."

Their partner might respond: "I understand that you're feeling insecure, but sometimes I need space to process my own emotions. I'm here for you, but we both need to find a balance."

Empathetic communication like this helps both partners to feel seen and understood, laying the groundwork for healing.

3. Set Realistic Expectations for Change

Change won't happen overnight, and that's okay. Repairing a relationship requires patience and ongoing effort. Both partners must be clear that while progress is possible, it will likely be gradual.

Setting small, realistic goals for the relationship is helpful, such as checking in regularly, practicing emotional regulation techniques, or scheduling time to reconnect without distractions. As each goal is achieved, it builds confidence that change is possible.

4. Focus on Building Trust and Consistency

Trust is often eroded in relationships affected by anxious attachment. Rebuilding trust requires both partners to be open, consistent, and willing to address the issues that have caused tension in the relationship.

The individual with anxious attachment can work on being more mindful of when they are feeling triggered and use coping mechanisms to manage their fears. At the same time, their partner can be more aware of providing reassurance in meaningful and authentic ways. Over time, as each partner demonstrates reliability, the relationship becomes more secure.

I've seen couples rebuild trust by focusing on small, consistent actions. One couple I worked with committed to having a monthly date night, free from distractions, to reconnect and rebuild their emotional intimacy. Over time, these consistent actions helped them create a stronger, more secure bond.

5. Seek Support When Needed

Repairing a relationship can sometimes be complex, especially when anxious attachment has caused significant strain. In these cases, seeking external support from a therapist or counselor can be incredibly beneficial. Professional guidance can provide both partners with tools and strategies to improve communication, navigate emotional challenges, and work through the underlying issues driving anxious attachment.

Couples therapy or individual therapy can also offer a safe space to explore difficult emotions, identify patterns, and develop healthier ways of relating to one another. The commitment to seeking help can strengthen the relationship and show both partners that they are invested in creating lasting change.

Repairing a relationship damaged by anxious attachment requires ongoing effort and intentionality. However, the rewards of this work are immense. As partners learn to navigate the complexities of their relationship with greater understanding and empathy, they build a resilient bond capable of weathering future challenges.

Repairing the relationship doesn't mean that the same worries and insecurities will never come up again. Instead, it means that both partners are better at handling those moments when they do. By continuing to communicate openly, set boundaries, and practice emotional regulation, the relationship can thrive on a foundation of trust, security, and mutual respect.

Ultimately, repairing a relationship damaged by anxious attachment is about choosing growth over fear, connection over avoidance, and healing over hurt. It's a testament to both partners' commitment to one another and their willingness to build a relationship that is not only secure but deeply fulfilling.

BUILDING A SECURE FOUNDATION

Building secure relationships is both demanding and life-changing. For someone recovering from anxious attachment, every step toward fostering emotional security—whether through choosing the right partner, setting healthy boundaries, or rebuilding trust—marks significant progress in your emotional growth. But this journey is not about perfection or getting it right every time. It's about embracing your inherent worth and acknowledging that you deserve relationships rooted in mutual respect, trust, and emotional intimacy.

Embrace your outlook with optimism. Take a moment to reflect on where you started and where you are now.

224

Each boundary you've set, each moment of emotional awareness, is a testament to your progress. Choosing to nurture yourself and your relationships creates a future where trust, love, and emotional security are not only possibilities but realities.

CHAPTER 9: RECLAIMING SELF-WORTH

At the core of anxious attachment often lies a fragile sense of self-worth. You may constantly question your value in relationships, feel unworthy of love, or doubt your ability to maintain a healthy connection. This lack of self-confidence can lead to a dependence on external validation, where your sense of worth is tied to how others perceive or treat you.

Reclaiming your self-worth is a critical step in overcoming anxious attachment and building emotional freedom. When you cultivate confidence from within, you free yourself from the need for constant reassurance and validation. You begin to trust that you are enough, that you are deserving of love and respect, and that your emotional well-being doesn't hinge on the approval or presence of others.

In this chapter, we'll explore practical ways to rebuild your self-worth, break free from self-doubt, and embrace emotional freedom.

REBUILDING SELF-ESTEEM

For individuals with anxious attachment, self-esteem can feel like a rollercoaster, heavily influenced by external validation. When your partner is attentive and affectionate, you may feel valued and secure. But when they're distant or unresponsive, your sense of worth can plummet, leaving you feeling inadequate and anxious. This reliance on external validation creates a fragile sense of self, constantly teetering on the edge of insecurity.

The constant need for reassurance and approval can keep you trapped in a cycle of self-doubt and insecurity. But the truth is, your worth is not something that fluctuates based on external

228

circumstances. It is inherent, unchanging, and independent of how others treat you.

Rebuilding self-esteem after experiencing anxious attachment means learning to shift your focus inward, recognizing your intrinsic value, and separating your sense of worth from external validation.

1. Acknowledge Your Worth

The first and most important step in rebuilding self-esteem is acknowledging your worth. Your value as a person does not come from how others perceive or treat you. You are inherently worthy simply because you exist. You deserve love, respect, and care regardless of whether someone else provides it for you.

It can be challenging to internalize this belief, especially if you've spent a lifetime seeking approval and validation from others. But the key to emotional freedom is realizing that your worth does not need to be earned or proven. It is a constant, unshakable truth.

One effective way to start acknowledging your worth is by reflecting on your personal strengths and qualities.

Take some time to think about what makes you unique, what you're proud of, and the positive attributes that define who you are. Shifting your focus from self-criticism to self-appreciation can transform the way you view yourself.

Exercise: Write a List of Your Strengths

Take a few moments to write down a list of your personal strengths, qualities, and achievements. Ask yourself the following questions:

- What makes me unique?

  Think about the characteristics, skills, or talents that set you apart from others. Whether it's your creativity, kindness, problem-solving abilities, or sense of humor, these qualities are what make you valuable.

- What am I proud of?

  Reflect on the accomplishments, big or small, that fill you with a sense of pride. These could include personal or professional achievements, moments of personal growth, or acts of kindness and generosity.

By focusing on your strengths and positive attributes, you can begin to shift your internal dialogue from one of self-doubt to one of self-appreciation. This exercise helps you see that your worth comes from who you are as a person, not from how others treat you or whether they offer validation.

2. Separate Your Self-Worth from External Validation

One of the major components of anxious attachment is the tendency to seek constant validation from others to feel secure. Whether it's asking for reassurance in a relationship, needing approval at work, or seeking compliments from friends, external validation becomes the measure by which you gauge your self-worth.

However, this reliance on external validation creates a cycle of dependency and insecurity. When others affirm you, you feel good about yourself, but when they don't, you begin to question your value. This rollercoaster can leave you emotionally drained and constantly anxious about whether you're "enough."

Rebuilding self-esteem involves separating your sense of worth from the opinions, reactions, and behaviors of others. It requires shifting from an external to an internal source of validation. While it's natural to enjoy praise or approval, your sense of self-worth should not be dependent on it.

Reflection: Do I Feel Worthy Only When Others Approve of Me?

Ask yourself the following questions to explore how you've been linking your self-worth to external validation:

- Do I only feel valuable when others compliment or validate me? Reflect on whether your sense of worth fluctuates based on the approval or disapproval of others. Do you feel good about yourself only when someone else recognizes your efforts or affirms your value?

- How can I affirm my value without needing external validation? Consider ways in which you can provide yourself with the validation you seek. Instead of waiting for others to approve of you, practice affirming yourself. Recognize your efforts, celebrate your achievements, and remind yourself of your inherent worth.

Example:

You're in a conversation with your partner, and they seem distracted. Suddenly, you find yourself spiraling into thoughts like 'They must be losing interest in me' or 'What did I do wrong?' The anxiety that follows stems from a deep-rooted belief that their behavior determines your worth. This pattern can play out in various relationships, from friendships to work dynamics, creating a constant need for reassurance. Recognizing these patterns and detaching your self-esteem from external validation is vital to emotional freedom.

Separating your self-worth from external validation means understanding that your value comes from within. It is not dependent on how others see you or what they say. Your worth is constant, whether or not someone else acknowledges it. As you begin to internalize this belief, you'll find that you are less affected by the ups and downs of external validation.

THE POWER OF POSITIVE SELF-TALK

A crucial step in reclaiming your self-worth is learning to cultivate a habit of positive self-talk. For individuals with anxious attachment, negative, self-critical thoughts often become deeply ingrained and automatic. These thoughts might sound like, "I'm not good enough," "I'll never be truly loved," or "I don't deserve happiness." Over time, this inner dialogue can chip away at your self-esteem, reinforcing the harmful belief that you are somehow lacking or unworthy.

But here's the truth: thoughts are not facts. Just because you've internalized these beliefs over time does not mean they are accurate reflections of who you are. Positive self-talk offers a powerful antidote to these negative patterns, helping you rewire your thinking and, in turn, rebuild your self-esteem.

Think of your mind like a garden. When you constantly feed it with negative thoughts, those thoughts take root and grow like weeds, spreading doubt and insecurity throughout your mental landscape. Positive self-talk, however, is like planting seeds of self-compassion and affirmation. The more you nurture these positive thoughts, the stronger they grow, crowding out the weeds of self-doubt.

It's important to realize that this transformation doesn't happen overnight. Just as weeds don't vanish with a single pull, negative thoughts won't disappear after a single positive affirmation. But with consistent effort, your inner dialogue will begin to shift from one of criticism and fear to one of encouragement and self-acceptance.

AFFIRMATIONS: REWRITING YOUR INNER NARRATIVE

One of the most effective ways to practice positive self-talk is through the use of affirmations—short, powerful statements that affirm your worth and potential. By consistently repeating these affirmations, you can gradually rewire your brain to think more positively and confidently. This can lead to increased self-esteem, reduced anxiety, and improved overall well-being.

Consider some of the common negative thoughts that arise from anxious attachment:

- **Negative Thought**: "I'm not good enough."
  - ○ **Affirmation**: "I am worthy just as I am. I have value that doesn't depend on anyone else's opinion."
- **Negative Thought**: "They'll leave me because I'm not worthy."

236

- o **Affirmation**: "I am deserving of love and respect. The right people will value and appreciate me for who I am."
- **Negative Thought**: "I always mess things up."
  - o **Affirmation**: "I am capable of growth and learning. Mistakes are part of my journey toward becoming stronger."

By consistently replacing negative thoughts with affirmations, you create new mental pathways—ones that are aligned with a growth mindset. Rather than being trapped in fixed beliefs that diminish your sense of worth, you begin to embrace the idea that your value is inherent and that you are capable of growth, healing, and change.

DEVELOPING A GROWTH MINDSET

The concept of a growth mindset—the belief that your abilities and qualities can be developed through effort, strategies, and help from others—

fits seamlessly into the practice of positive self-talk. A growth mindset allows you to move away from the fear of failure and rejection, which often fuels anxious attachment, and toward a mindset of possibility and resilience.

When you encounter challenges, setbacks, or emotional triggers, positive self-talk, coupled with a growth mindset, can help you reframe these experiences as opportunities for learning rather than evidence of your inadequacy. For example:

- Instead of saying, "I'm a failure because this relationship isn't working," you might affirm, "I am learning and growing through every experience. Each step brings me closer to the healthy relationship I deserve."
- Instead of thinking, "I'll never be able to change," you can tell yourself, "I am capable of growth, and with time and effort, I can create the emotional security I need."

A growth mindset helps you view your journey of self-worth as ongoing and dynamic. It reinforces the idea that you are not defined by past patterns or mistakes but by your willingness to evolve and embrace new ways of thinking. Each affirmation becomes a small step toward this evolution, helping you release limiting beliefs and cultivate emotional freedom.

I used to believe that my social anxiety was a fixed trait, something I was simply "stuck with." This belief prevented me from putting myself out there and forming new connections. But when I embraced a growth mindset, I started to see my anxiety as a challenge I could overcome. With practice and support, I gradually stepped outside my comfort zone, and each small victory fueled my belief in my ability to grow and change.

PRACTICAL TIPS FOR PRACTICING POSITIVE SELF-TALK

1. **Consistency is Key**: Rewriting your inner narrative takes time and persistence. Make positive self-talk a daily practice by starting your day with affirmations or repeating them whenever you feel self-doubt creeping in. The more frequently you engage with positive self-talk, the more natural it becomes.

2. **Be Specific and Present**: When creating affirmations, make them specific and grounded in the present moment. Instead of saying, "I will be confident," try "I am becoming more confident every day." This helps anchor the affirmation in your current reality and affirms the progress you're already making.

3. **Write It Down**: Writing down your affirmations can help reinforce them. Keep a journal where you document your

affirmations and reflect on how they've helped you reshape your thoughts over time. Repetition is a powerful tool, and seeing your affirmations in writing can make them feel more tangible.

4. **Pair with Visualization**: To amplify the power of positive self-talk, pair your affirmations with visualization. As you repeat your affirmations, imagine yourself embodying the qualities you're affirming. Visualize yourself feeling confident, secure, and worthy in your relationships and interactions. This practice helps make your affirmations feel real and achievable.

As you integrate positive self-talk into your life, remember that this is not about eliminating every negative thought overnight. It's about progress, not perfection. Every time you catch yourself in a negative spiral and consciously choose to replace those thoughts with affirming, growth-oriented ones, you are making strides toward reclaiming your self-worth.

This practice is an essential part of your journey toward emotional freedom. The more you nurture these affirmations, the more you'll begin to believe in your inherent worth, independent of external validation. With time, you'll find that positive self-talk doesn't just reshape your inner dialogue—it reshapes how you show up in the world, how you respond to challenges, and how you build healthy, secure relationships grounded in self-confidence and love.

BREAKING THE CYCLE OF SELF-DOUBT

While a growth mindset is a powerful tool, overcoming self-doubt often requires actively confronting and dismantling those deep-seated negative thought patterns. Let's explore how to break free from this cycle and cultivate unwavering self-belief.

Self-doubt is a persistent and often crippling challenge for individuals with anxious attachment. It can infiltrate every area of life, from your personal

242

relationships to your professional endeavors, making you question your abilities, decisions, and even your worth as a person. This constant second-guessing can erode your confidence, leaving you feeling inadequate and reinforcing the belief that you are not enough. But the cycle of self-doubt, while powerful, is not unbreakable.

At its core, self-doubt is driven by negative thought patterns—thoughts and beliefs that undermine your sense of self-worth and create barriers to personal growth. These thoughts often stem from insecurities formed in early relationships and are reinforced by repeated patterns of seeking external validation. However, by learning to challenge these thoughts and adopting a mindset rooted in self-compassion, you can begin to break free from the grip of self-doubt and cultivate a stronger, more confident sense of self.

1. Challenge Negative Thought Patterns

Self-doubt thrives on negative thought patterns—those automatic thoughts that tell you that you're not good enough, that you'll never succeed, or that you're unworthy of love and respect. These thoughts become

243

deeply ingrained over time, especially for individuals with anxious attachment who may have internalized feelings of inadequacy from inconsistent caregiving or past relationships. Left unchecked, these negative thought patterns create a cycle of self-sabotage, making it difficult to trust yourself and your decisions.

To break the cycle of self-doubt, you must first become aware of these thoughts and actively challenge them. The goal is to shift from a mindset of self-criticism to one of self-affirmation by questioning the validity of the negative beliefs that fuel your doubts.

How to Challenge Negative Thoughts:

- Is this thought based on fact, or is it a result of my   insecurities? One of the most effective ways to challenge self-doubt is to examine the evidence behind your negative thoughts. When you find yourself thinking, "I'm not good enough," or "I always mess things up," ask yourself if this belief is truly based on facts or if it's simply a reflection of your insecurities. Often, you'll find that these thoughts are not rooted in reality but are driven by fear and past experiences.

- What evidence do I have to support or refute this   belief? Take a step back and objectively assess the situation. What concrete evidence do you have to support the belief that you're inadequate or that you'll fail? More often than not, you'll find that there's very little evidence to justify these negative thoughts. By focusing on the facts rather than the fear, you can begin to shift your perspective and realize that your self-doubt may not be as justified as it feels.

- What would I say to a friend who was thinking this   way? When you're stuck in a cycle of self-doubt, it's easy to be harder on yourself than you would be on others. Imagine that a close friend is experiencing the same thoughts of doubt and insecurity. What would you say to them? Would you criticize them for feeling this way, or would you offer them compassion and reassurance? Use this same kind and understanding approach with yourself. By treating yourself as you would a friend, you can soften the harshness of your inner critic and begin to develop a more supportive inner dialogue.

Example:

Imagine you're at work and you've made a small mistake. Instantly, the inner critic kicks in: 'I'm not good at this,' or 'I'll never be successful.' Before you know it, your mind is spiraling into worst-case scenarios. In this moment, you need to challenge the thought: What is the evidence that I'm not good at my job? Have I made mistakes before and recovered? Reminding yourself of past successes helps shift your thinking from failure to growth.

2. Practice Self-Compassion

One of the most powerful antidotes to self-doubt is self-compassion. At the root of self-doubt is often a harsh inner critic—a voice that judges you for every mistake, perceives every shortcoming as a failure, and holds you to an impossible standard of perfection. This inner critic feeds on your insecurities and fuels the belief that you are not enough. The practice of self-compassion, however, offers a different path—a path of kindness, patience, and understanding toward yourself.

Self-compassion means treating yourself with the same care and consideration that you would offer to someone you love. It's about recognizing that you are human, that everyone makes mistakes, and that your worth is not diminished by imperfection. Self-compassion allows you to embrace your flaws without judgment and to offer yourself the grace and encouragement needed to grow.

How to Practice Self-Compassion:

- Speak to Yourself with Kindness:

  Notice when self-critical thoughts arise and gently replace them with words of kindness and encouragement. For example, if you find yourself thinking, "I'm such a failure," shift that thought to something more compassionate, like "I did my best, and it's okay to make mistakes." This practice may feel uncomfortable at first, especially if you're used to harsh self-judgment, but over time, it will become more natural to speak to yourself with kindness.

- Acknowledge Your Humanity:

  It's important to remember that everyone experiences moments of self-doubt, setbacks, and challenges. You are not alone in your struggles, and your worth is not defined by your mistakes. By acknowledging your shared humanity, you can begin to release the unrealistic expectation that you need to be perfect in order to be worthy. Embrace the idea that imperfection is part of the human experience, and that it's okay to be a work in progress.

- Be Patient with Yourself:

  Building self-esteem and confidence is a journey, and it takes time to break the cycle of self-doubt. Be patient with yourself as you work through your doubts and insecurities.

Celebrate the small victories—each time you challenge a negative thought or offer yourself a moment of kindness, you are taking a step toward greater self-compassion and confidence. Progress may be slow, but each step forward is a sign of growth.

Breaking the cycle of self-doubt requires both a shift in mindset and a commitment to self-compassion. By challenging the negative thoughts that undermine your confidence and treating yourself with the kindness and understanding you deserve, you can begin to free yourself from the grip of self-doubt. Over time, this practice will help you develop a more secure and resilient sense of self-worth—one that is not easily shaken by external circumstances or the judgments of others.

As you cultivate self-compassion and challenge the patterns of self-doubt, you will find that your confidence grows, and your sense of worth becomes more grounded in your own intrinsic value. This newfound confidence will ripple into your relationships, allowing you to approach them with greater trust, emotional security, and self-assurance.

249

Self-Care as a Foundation for Security

Self-care is an essential part of building self-worth and emotional resilience. When you prioritize self-care, you send a powerful message to yourself: I am worthy of love, care, and attention. Self-care is holistic, encompassing all aspects of your health, including physical, emotional, mental, and spiritual well-being.

1. Establish a Self-Care Routine

Creating a consistent self-care routine helps reinforce the belief that you are deserving of care and attention. This routine can include activities that nourish your body, mind, and soul.

Examples of Self-Care Activities:

- Physical Care: Engage in regular exercise, get enough sleep, and eat nourishing foods that support your physical well-being.
- Emotional Care: Practice mindfulness, journaling, or meditation to help manage

stress and connect with your emotions. Take time to process your feelings in a healthy way, rather than suppressing them or relying on others for validation.

- Social Care: Surround yourself with supportive people who uplift and encourage you. Spend time with friends and loved ones who respect your boundaries and contribute positively to your life.

2. Honor Your Needs and Boundaries

Part of self-care is learning to honor your own needs and boundaries. When you set boundaries, you protect your emotional well-being and ensure that your relationships are based on mutual respect and understanding.

How to Honor Your Needs:

- Recognize Your Limits: Be aware of your emotional, physical, and mental limits. If you're feeling overwhelmed, stressed, or emotionally drained, give yourself permission to step back and recharge.

- Communicate Your Boundaries: Let others know when you need space, time, or support. Communicating your boundaries clearly and respectfully helps others understand your needs and shows that you value yourself.
- Say No When Necessary: Saying no is an act of self-care. It's okay to decline requests or commitments that don't align with your well-being. By saying no when necessary, you free up time and energy for the things that truly matter to you.

EMBRACING EMOTIONAL FREEDOM

Emotional freedom is the ability to navigate your emotions with confidence and resilience. It's about trusting that you can handle whatever life throws your way without being overwhelmed by fear, doubt, or insecurity. Emotional freedom comes from a deep sense of self-worth and the belief that you are capable of managing your emotions, regardless of external circumstances.

1. Cultivate Emotional Independence

Emotional independence means that you no longer rely on others to provide you with a sense of security or validation. While relationships can offer support and comfort, true emotional freedom comes from within.

How to Cultivate Emotional Independence:

- Develop Healthy Coping Mechanisms: Instead of seeking reassurance from others, practice healthy coping mechanisms to manage your emotions. This could include mindfulness, deep breathing, or journaling.
- Trust Your Inner Strength: Remind yourself that you are capable of handling difficult emotions. Trust that you have the inner strength to navigate challenges, even when things feel uncertain.
- Let Go of Control: Emotional freedom also involves letting go of the need to control others or the outcome of situations. Accept that you can't control everything, but you can control how you respond.

253

2. Celebrate Your Progress

As you work toward emotional freedom, it's important to celebrate your progress along the way. Recognize the steps you've taken to build your self-worth, challenge self-doubt, and cultivate emotional independence. Each small victory is a testament to your growth and resilience.

Take time to reflect on how far you've come in your journey toward secure attachment. Celebrate the moments when you stood up for yourself, practiced self-compassion, or trusted in your own worth. These moments are evidence that you are reclaiming your emotional freedom and stepping into a more confident, secure version of yourself.

By building self-confidence, practicing self-care, and embracing emotional independence, you can overcome the patterns of anxious attachment and create a life grounded in inner security.

As you develop a strong sense of self-worth, you will notice a shift in how you respond to emotional triggers. Instead of reacting with anxiety or doubt when faced with conflict or perceived rejection, you will feel grounded, knowing that your worth is not tied to others' behaviors or opinions. This is emotional freedom—the confidence that you can handle any emotional challenge because you trust yourself and your inherent value.

CONCLUSION: THE ROAD TO LASTING SECURITY

As we conclude this book, it's time to reflect on the transformative journey you've undertaken. The path from anxious to secure attachment is deeply personal and often challenging, yet the rewards are profound. By engaging with the insights and practices offered in these pages, you've made a powerful commitment to your emotional growth, well-being, and relationship health.

More than just a guide, this book has been your companion as you navigated the complexities of anxious attachment, developed new ways of understanding yourself, and cultivated the tools

257

needed for healthier relationships. Though this book may be ending, your journey is just beginning. The knowledge, self-awareness, and practical strategies you've gained will continue to serve as the foundation for a life filled with emotional security, meaningful connections, and an enduring sense of self-worth.

While not achieved overnight, this transformation is a testament to your courage and strength. You've confronted your fears, embraced vulnerability, and developed the skills to manage your emotions with greater confidence and resilience. Armed with a deeper self-awareness and the tools to foster secure relationships, you stand on the edge of a brighter future.

Remember, the fears of rejection, abandonment, and inadequacy that often accompany anxious attachment do not have to define you or your relationships. As you've learned throughout this book, emotional freedom comes when you refuse to let these fears dictate your actions, thoughts, or self-worth.

I recall the countless nights I spent agonizing over perceived slights and unanswered texts, feeling stuck in a cycle of anxiety and self-doubt. It required courage and vulnerability to confront those fears and commit to change, but the rewards have been immeasurable. Like me, you can also overcome the challenges of anxious attachment and create a life filled with secure love and lasting confidence.

It's important to embrace the process rather than fixating on the end goal. True transformation lies in the growth you experience through each practice of self-compassion, each boundary set, and each step toward emotional independence. Be patient with yourself, and celebrate each victory along the way, no matter how small. Each step forward is progress, and that progress is worth celebrating.

By trusting in your own worth and validating your feelings, you're building the foundation for lasting emotional freedom—a life where secure relationships and genuine well-being flourish.

While this book has primarily focused on romantic relationships, the principles of secure attachment and emotional healing apply to every area of your life. The skills you've developed—self-regulation, communication, and boundary-setting—will empower you to build fulfilling connections in friendships, family relationships, and professional settings.

Secure attachment extends far beyond romance; it's about creating trust, safety, and mutual respect in all relationships. The self-worth and emotional independence you've cultivated empower you to navigate friendships, family relationships, and workplace dynamics with confidence and clarity. Remember, the insights you've gained here will continue to support you as you build fulfilling connections in every area of your life.

As you move forward, keep embracing each step of your growth, and let your newfound sense of emotional security guide you into even deeper connections and a more peaceful, fulfilled life.

You've come so far, and there's still so much ahead. Trust in the process, trust in your worth, and trust that you're fully capable of building the life and relationships you deserve.

Take a moment to recognize the courage you've shown in this journey. Every insight gained, every step taken, is a testament to your strength and worth. By engaging with this book, you've demonstrated immense bravery and commitment to your emotional well-being. You've taken the first steps toward transforming not only your relationships but also your mindset and your sense of self.

Stay curious, stay open, and prioritize your emotional well-being. Each step you take, no matter how small, brings you closer to greater emotional freedom, stronger relationships, and deeper inner peace. Emotional security is within your reach, and you're already on your way toward making that a reality.

Continue to nurture your self-worth, embrace your emotional resilience, and seek out supportive communities or resources that can further aid your growth. You're capable of lasting emotional security, and the journey toward that reality is ongoing. Embrace it with courage, compassion, and an unwavering belief in your own worthiness.

ONE MORE THING!

If you enjoyed this book and found it helpful, I'd be very grateful if you'd post a short review on Amazon. Your support does make a difference, and I read all the reviews personally so I can get your feedback and make this book even better. I love hearing from my readers, and I'd really appreciate it if you leave your honest feedback.

Thank you for reading!

BONUS CHAPTER

I would like to share a sneak peek into another one of my books that I think you will enjoy. The book is titled **_"The Path to Secure Attachment: Transforming Anxious and Avoidant Patterns into Secure Relationships, and Leveraging Attachment Theory for Healthy Relationships and Emotional Intelligence."_**

Do you yearn for deeper connection, but find yourself trapped in cycles of frustration and longing?

"The Path to Secure Attachment" is your guide to

263

transforming your relationships, breaking free from unhealthy patterns, and embracing the fulfilling love you deserve.

Building upon the insights of *"Anxious Attachment and Avoidant Detachment,"* this book delves into the heart of secure attachment – the cornerstone of healthy, thriving relationships. Discover how to cultivate the safety, trust, and balanced emotional connection that fosters lasting love.

Your Transformation Starts Here

Understand the profound impact of your earliest experiences on your adult relationships. Uncover the neurobiology of attachment: how your brain forms bonds and how this impacts the way you navigate intimacy. Learn how to recognize your own attachment style and those of others, unlocking a deeper understanding of your behaviors and relationship dynamics.

This book is your roadmap to transform insecure attachment patterns into a secure, balanced state. Develop the skills essential for fulfilling connection:

- **Master Effective Communication:** Express your needs with clarity and compassion, and learn to truly listen to your partner.
- **Cultivate Emotional Intelligence:** Decode your emotions and those of your partner, creating a space for understanding and empathy.
- **Build Unshakeable Trust:** Overcome past hurts and learn to rely on your partner for support and comfort.
- **Nurture Self-Compassion:** Embrace your strengths and weaknesses, offering yourself the same kindness you extend to loved ones.

The Benefits Extend Far Beyond Your Romantic Life

265

Secure attachment is the foundation for strong connections across all areas of your life. Learn how to:

- **Strengthen Friendships and Family Bonds:** Apply the same principles of empathy and clear communication to deepen all your relationships.

- **Become a Secure Base for Your Children:** Raise emotionally healthy children by providing them with the secure attachment they need to thrive.

- **Enhance Workplace Collaboration:** Build stronger rapport with colleagues, approach conflict with confidence, and cultivate a sense of belonging within your team.

- **Improve Your Relationship with Yourself:** Develop greater self-awareness, treat yourself with compassion, and set healthy boundaries.

- **Boost Overall Well-being:** Experience reduced stress, increased resilience in facing challenges, and a greater sense of personal fulfillment.
- **Navigate the World with Confidence:** Secure attachment fosters a sense of safety and security, allowing you to explore new experiences, take healthy risks, and approach challenges with greater ease.

Don't settle for a life of missed connections and unfulfilled relationships. "The Path to Secure Attachment" empowers you to break free from the past and build the future you desire – a future filled with resilient love, mutual support, and deep, lasting connection.

Seize this opportunity for growth. Buy your copy today and embark on a journey towards secure, fulfilling relationships.

Enjoy this free chapter!

267

We all yearn for secure, supportive connections—they're the foundation upon which we thrive. This journey promises new insights into the intricate world of relationships and deeper self-understanding. Whether the prequel, Anxious Attachment and Avoidant Detachment, inspired deeper introspection and sparked your curiosity, or this is your first exploration of attachment theory's impact on relationships, your engagement with these pages is vital. This sequel builds upon the foundation of the prequel, expanding your understanding and offering new insights, deeper explorations, and practical guidance for nurturing secure, healthy relationships. *The only way to live is to grow - And that journey of growth includes how we form and nurture relationships.*

Understanding attachment is an ongoing journey of self-discovery and growth. "In the prequel, I explored the patterns of anxious and avoidant attachments, revealing how these early bonds shape our adult relationships. Now, we focus on the cornerstone of resilient relationships: secure attachment. This book will empower you with practical tools to foster security and stability in all your relationships. While the prequel exposed the challenges of insecure attachment, this book provides the path toward healing and change.

Secure attachment is more than just a theory; it embodies a state of emotional balance, mutual respect, and understanding. It means feeling comfortable asking for support, working through conflict calmly, and celebrating each other's successes. It's about forming connections that aren't only enduring but also supportive and enriching. As we embark on this new phase of our journey together, we'll explore the principles of secure attachment, understand its implications for our daily lives, and learn how to cultivate and maintain these healthy bonds.

This book is structured to be both a reflection of

your journey and a guide for your path ahead. Each chapter builds upon the insights and lessons from the prequel, providing a deeper understanding of attachment styles and offering practical strategies for nurturing secure relationships. Whether you're seeking personal growth, healing from past relationships, or looking to strengthen your current bonds, this book is designed to meet you where you are and guide you forward.

As you begin this exploration, remember that each page, concept, and strategy contributes to a larger journey—one of understanding, growth, and connection. This book isn't just a set of pages to be read; it's a journey to be experienced, a path to be walked, and your story of transformation.

Together, we'll delve into secure attachment, understanding its theory and the practical, life-changing ways it can manifest in our lives and relationships. Let's turn the page – a new chapter of possibility and transformation begins.

Think of this book as a dialogue with your innermost self. These pages mirror your experiences, aspirations, and the intricate dynamics of your relationships. This is where your journey intersects with the collective narrative of those striving for secure, meaningful, and enriching connections. This book is your companion, guide, and confidant as you navigate the intricacies of building nurturing and enduring relationships.

Prepare to be challenged, inspired, and transformed. Remember that every insight gained is a step forward. Every reflection deepens your understanding. Every strategy applied is a tool for forging stronger, more resilient, and more fulfilling bonds. This is an expansion of your horizons, a deepening of your insights, and a celebration of the journey that each of us is on— toward understanding ourselves, our attachments, and the web of relationships that we weave throughout our lives.

As we focus on nurturing secure attachment, let's revisit the foundational concepts of attachment theory explored in the prequel. This theory—a cornerstone of understanding emotional bonds—provides invaluable insights into the intricacies of human relationships. It's about how we relate to others, and understanding the deep-seated patterns that guide our interactions and shape our emotional landscape of trust and vulnerability.

Attachment theory, pioneered by John Bowlby and expanded by Mary Ainsworth and others, shows us how the bonds formed between a child and their primary caregivers set the stage for future relationship dynamics. These early interactions establish patterns for how individuals perceive themselves and others, influencing their sense of security, their ability to form and maintain emotional bonds, and their response to intimacy and dependency.

The theory categorizes attachment into four distinct styles:

1. **Anxious Attachment (sometimes referred to as "Preoccupied"):**
   - Develops from inconsistent caregiving and emotional availability.
   - Results in adults who seek high levels of intimacy, approval, and responsiveness from partners, often fearing rejection or abandonment.

2. **Avoidant Attachment (sometimes referred to as "Dismissive"):**
   - Arises from caregivers who are emotionally unavailable or unresponsive.
   - Leads to adults who are self-sufficient to the point of pushing others away, often prioritizing independence over intimacy.

3. **Disorganized Attachment (sometimes referred to as "Fearful-Avoidant"):**

- Usually stems from trauma or severe inconsistency in caregiving.
- Results in adults who desire close relationships but find it hard to trust or depend on others completely.

4. **Secure Attachment:**
   - Originates from consistent, responsive caregiving.
   - Leads to adults with a positive view of themselves, their partners, and their relationships.
   - Characterized by comfort with intimacy as well as independence to create balanced and healthy relationships.

Understanding these styles is crucial as they provide a framework for examining our own behaviors and preferences in relationships. Recognizing one's own attachment style can be deeply illuminating, offering explanations for feelings and behaviors that previously seemed confusing. It empowers individuals to navigate their relationships more mindfully, understand their own needs, and empathize with those of their partners.

We'll revisit these attachment theory concepts by viewing them as building blocks for the chapters ahead. They serve as the framework through which we delve into the intricacies and principles of secure attachment, offering a comprehensive and enlightened foundation for the practical strategies and insights presented in this book.

In exploring secure attachment, we embrace the evolving nature of relationships, knowing that challenges, life changes, and growth are all part of the journey. Secure attachment isn't about achieving a state of perfection; it's about cultivating a sense of balance, understanding, and mutual respect. It's about creating a foundation of security within ourselves. This security radiates outward, enriching all our relationships.

276

We'll delve into the interplay between self-awareness, empathy, and communication – essential elements for secure, healthy relationships. This exploration isn't just theoretical; it's practical and deeply personal. It's about bringing the principles of secure attachment to life and making them a living reality in your day-to-day interactions.

Whether you're seeking healing, growth, or to help others, this book offers a structured path with insights, reflections, and exercises to support you every step of the way. It's intended to be a living document in your life that you can consult, reflect upon, and draw insights from over time. Here's how to maximize the value you get from it:

1. **Engage Deeply for Maximum Impact**
   - Read actively, not mindlessly. Engage with the material by considering how it applies to your personal experiences. Reflect on the concepts and theories

presented and relate them to your own life.

2. **Explore, Reflect, and Grow**

- Take your time with each chapter, allowing the ideas to sink in. Reflect on how the information might change your understanding of your past interactions and how it might influence your future ones. Use the book as a journal of sorts, making notes in the margins or in a separate notebook where you can write down thoughts, feelings, and revelations.

3. **Put Your Learning into Action**

- Gradually implement the insights and strategies you learn in your life. Change is a process; lasting transformation occurs through consistent, intentional practice over time. Focus on one concept or strategy at a time, and observe how it influences your relationships and your perspective on attachment.

4. **Find Support and Share Insights**

- Use the book as a conversation starter with friends, family, or a therapist. Discussing your insights and challenges with others can provide new perspectives and deepen your understanding of the material.

5. **Your Evolving Companion**

- Your relationship with this book should evolve alongside you. Different sections may become more relevant or have new meanings as you grow and change. Make it a habit to revisit parts that struck a chord with you or that you found particularly challenging, and see if your new experiences shed new light on them.

6. **Embrace Patience on Your Journey**

- The journey to understanding and fostering secure attachment in your life isn't linear. It will have its ups and downs – days when insights feel clear, and days when old patterns resurface. Approach this journey with patience and compassion for yourself. Change takes time, and self-growth is a continuous, often nonlinear process.

The insights and strategies within these pages hold the greatest potential for transformation when reflected upon and applied to your unique life experiences. The heartfelt application of these ideas will foster the growth and development of more secure, enriching relationships in your life.

View each chapter as an opportunity to deepen your understanding of yourself and your relationships. Let this book be a companion and a guide as you navigate the complex yet rewarding path toward secure attachment and relational fulfillment. It recognizes that the pursuit of secure attachment isn't confined to a particular relationship status or life stage. Whether you're single, immersed in the complexities of dating, deeply rooted in a long-term partnership, or fostering familial and platonic bonds. The principles of secure attachment are universally applicable, offering the potential for transformation at every stage of life.

The journey toward secure attachment is as individual as it is universal. While each person's journey is unique – shaped by past experiences and individual goals – our underlying need for connection and growth binds us together.

For those who are single, this book sheds light on the patterns that have defined past relationships and offers a framework for building future connections with intention and clarity. It gives you the knowledge to understand your attachment style, identify red flags early on, and lay the groundwork for partnerships built upon mutual growth and support.

For individuals in relationships, the insights within these pages provide a deeper understanding of your own and your partner's attachment styles. This knowledge is powerful—it transforms communication, aids conflict resolution, and strengthens the bonds of intimacy and trust. It's about nurturing a relationship that's both enduring and deeply fulfilling, offering a safe space for both individuals to grow and flourish.

Parents will find in this book a valuable resource for shaping their children's communication styles, conflict resolution skills, and capacity for trust. The principles of secure attachment, when introduced early in life, can cultivate the seeds for future relationships that are healthy, resilient, and fulfilling. It's about creating an environment that fosters emotional intelligence, empathy, and a deep sense of security from the earliest stages of development.

Furthermore, this book extends its reach beyond

282

individual relationships to the broader community. It sparks the creation of supportive networks where individuals can share experiences, offer support, and grow together. It's a call to build a community that values emotional intelligence, mutual respect, and collective well-being.

As you progress through this book, remember that the path to secure attachment, though personal, echoes the universal human quest for connection, understanding, and growth. Each step forward not only enriches your own life, but ripples outward - contributing to a world where everyone feels capable of healthy, supportive, and transformative relationships.

Embrace the journey that this book invites you to embark upon. Let it guide you toward deeper, more meaningful connections in every facet of your life. Through individual growth and shared understanding, we can cultivate a world where secure attachment isn't just an ideal but a lived reality, where every relationship is an opportunity for mutual support, profound connection, and enduring growth.

Get your full copy today!

BEST SELLERS BY RICHARD BANKS

Assertiveness Training: Learn How to Say No and Stop People-Pleasing by Establishing Healthy Boundaries

The Keys to Being Brilliantly Confident and More Assertive: A Vital Guide to Enhancing Your Communication Skills, Getting Rid of Anxiety, and Building Assertiveness

The Art of Active Listening: How to Listen Effectively in 10 Simple Steps to Improve Relationships and Increase Productivity

How to Deal With Stress, Depression, and Anxiety: A Vital Guide on How to Deal with Nerves and Coping with Stress, Pain, OCD and Trauma

How to Deal with Grief, Loss, and Death: A Survivor's Guide to Coping with Pain and Trauma, and Learning to Live Again

Develop a Positive Mindset and Attract the Life of Your Dreams: Unleash Positive Thinking to Achieve Unbound Happiness, Health, and Success

How to Stop Being Negative, Angry, and Mean: Master Your Mind and Take Control of Your Life

For the Full Book Listing go to

https://author.to/RichardBanksBooks

REFERENCES

Ainsworth, M. D. S., Blehar, M. C., Waters, E., & Wall, S. (1978). *Patterns of Attachment: A Psychological Study of the Strange Situation*. Erlbaum.

Bowlby, J. (1982). *Attachment and Loss: Vol. 1. Attachment* (2nd ed.). Basic Books.

Brown, B. (2012). *Daring Greatly: How the Courage to Be Vulnerable Transforms the Way We Live, Love, Parent, and Lead*. Gotham Books.

Cloud, H., & Townsend, J. (1992). *Boundaries: When to Say Yes, How to Say No to Take Control of Your Life*. Zondervan.

Goleman, D. (1995). *Emotional Intelligence: Why It Can Matter More Than IQ*. Bantam Books.

Hazan, C., & Shaver, P. R. (1987). Romantic love conceptualized as an attachment process. *Journal of Personality and Social Psychology, 52*(3), 511-524. https://doi.org/10.1037/0022-3514.52.3.511

Johnson, S. M. (2008). *Hold Me Tight: Seven Conversations for a Lifetime of Love*. Little, Brown Spark.

287

Levine, A., & Heller, R. (2010). *Attached: The New Science of Adult Attachment and How It Can Help You Find—and Keep—Love*. TarcherPerigee.

Mikulincer, M., & Shaver, P. R. (2007). *Attachment in Adulthood: Structure, Dynamics, and Change*. Guilford Press.

Siegel, D. J. (2011). *The Developing Mind: How Relationships and the Brain Interact to Shape Who We Are* (2nd ed.). Guilford Press.

Tatkin, S. (2016). *Wired for Dating: How Understanding Neurobiology and Attachment Style Can Help You Find Your Ideal Mate*. New Harbinger Publications.

Tatkin, S. (2011). *Wired for Love: How Understanding Your Partner's Brain and Attachment Style Can Help You Defuse Conflict and Build a Secure Relationship*. New Harbinger Publications.

Zeanah, C. H. (2000). *Handbook of Infant Mental Health* (2nd ed.). Guilford Press.

Printed in Dunstable, United Kingdom